Barcode in Back

D1794487

3199 Lakeshore Blvd. West
Toronto, ON   M8V 1K8

BEING FEMALE

BEING FEMALE

The Continuum of Sexualization

Jennifer K. Wesely

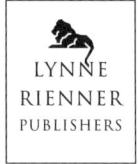
LYNNE
RIENNER
PUBLISHERS

BOULDER
LONDON

Published in the United States of America in 2012 by
Lynne Rienner Publishers, Inc.
1800 30th Street, Boulder, Colorado 80301
www.rienner.com

and in the United Kingdom by
Lynne Rienner Publishers, Inc.
3 Henrietta Street, Covent Garden, London WC2E 8LU

© 2012 by Lynne Rienner Publishers, Inc. All rights reserved

Library of Congress Cataloging-in-Publication Data
Wesely, Jennifer K.
　Being female : the continuum of sexualization / Jennifer K. Wesely.
　　p. cm.
　Includes bibliographical references and index.
　ISBN 978-1-58826-832-7 (hbk. : alk. paper)
　1. Sex role. 2. Sexism. 3. Sex crimes. 4. Women—Identity.
　5. Women—Sexual behavior. I. Title.
　HQ1075.W46 2012
　305.3—dc23
　　　　　　　　　　　　　　　　　　　　　　　2011034703

British Cataloguing in Publication Data
A Cataloguing in Publication record for this book
is available from the British Library.

Printed and bound in the United States of America

∞　The paper used in this publication meets the requirements
　of the American National Standard for Permanence of
　Paper for Printed Library Materials Z39.48-1992.

5 4 3 2 1

To
Octavia, Peaches, my niece, Fiona, and
all the other girls and young women who will be the next generation—
you inspire my efforts to make this world a better place

And to
Kevin, my love

Contents

1	The Continuum of Sexualization	1
2	Gender Socialization in Today's Culture	7
3	The Processes of Sexualization	33
4	Personal and Social Consequences	55
5	Tracing Pathways to Victimization	83
6	How Can We Stop Failing Girls and Women?	109
7	A Challenge to Our Society	135

Appendix: Methods for Qualitative Interviews	147
Bibliography	151
Index	163
About the Book	171

BEING FEMALE

1

The Continuum of Sexualization

I always wanted to be a boy. I was a tomboy. When I was younger I wanted to be a boy. I think it was because I wanted to be my brother, 'cause my parents favored him. But being a girl, I just learned . . . you don't learn it unless someone teaches you, and that's how the world works, you don't just know things. Everything is taught to you. And I just learned, I don't know how old I was, but I learned that people only paid attention to me because I was cute, or because I was sexy . . . when I go to the store, flirt a little bit, or wear a low-cut shirt, and you know they're looking. Or, the tight jeans or something . . . I don't know where I learned that along the way. —*Rita, age 21*

Rita tells me this during a late afternoon conversation that takes place in an empty conference room on a college campus. At the time, I am a PhD candidate completing research for my doctoral dissertation. Rita is putting herself through college. As we talk, Rita's demeanor is one of nonchalance. She is casual when it comes to what she has learned about being a girl in the world. She is tough. I am to think that this does not faze her; that she has taken what she has learned and turned it on its head, made the most of it, capitalized on it. Rita works as an exotic dancer.

A few weeks later, I meet up with her at the club on a Tuesday. As it is a weeknight, it's slow, and Rita goes into a stage performance directed toward one of the few customers, a man sitting alone right in front of the stage. Her smile is very different from how it appeared earlier. It is empty, a void. She arches her back and takes her legs, with spiked heels, and wraps them around the customer's neck. With her legs like this, she gyrates her hips in simulated sex rhythm. As I watch her perform in this contorted position, I remember part of our conversation from the campus conference room, when she was telling me about how she started dancing in the first place:

> My mom had no money. She had none. She never worked, she was kind of a trophy wife. I hate to say that but she raised children and stayed at home and was really beautiful, and young, and that was kind of her lifestyle. Never went to college. And then everything split up and she had nowhere else to turn and she's already borrowed money from relatives. And my account, I was 18, and she could say, well, I'm her mother, I'm just taking it out for her. In her mind, "I'm just going to borrow it and pay it back." That's fine if she's going to pay it back but . . . where's she going to get it from? Nowhere. She has no money. This month she called me, "I need money."
>
> The whole reason I got into this was because I had no money left and I had nothing else to do, and some sorority sister of mine thought it would be kinky and fun to go into a strip club and just try it for the fun of it. We sat there for two hours, the manager was like, "ooh, cute sorority girls, we could sell these girls for a pretty penny."
>
> The first time I went on stage they had someone ask me for a lap dance. Practically in tears I was so scared. You just don't know. And I'd never even had sex before, and I'm up here faking noises on stage, and trying to be all sexy, like I have any idea what's going on. It took a long time for me to practice and watch, and that's the only way you learn that.

When she describes her struggle to start working at the strip club, and as she also mentions her real-life lack of sexual experience, I am deeply disturbed by the fact that Rita's personal sexual growth and adjustment are eclipsed and cheapened by strip club parody. But that is not the first time she has learned to act sexualized. Just as effectively as in the club, she was schooled in this everyday art early on. What she describes learning is that when it comes to being female, it is the sexualized performance that matters.

The Continuum of Sexualization Concept

Two major research projects thus far in my career have involved in-depth interviews with separate groups of women, those who worked as exotic dancers and those who experienced homelessness (see the Appendix for more information). As I listened to the stories of Rita and many others for more than a decade, I was haunted by certain consistencies across their narratives. As this started to take shape and solidify for me, I felt a growing urgency to identify and articulate these consistencies. They became known to me as the "continuum of sexualization." Though I initially developed this concept based on patterns that persisted among women in my own research, it has far greater reach. Beyond the original conceptualization, I argue that it is applicable to the complicated array of lived experiences among the broader population of girls and women. It is true that the populations of which my study participants were members inhabited the "margins" of society, typically appearing invisible to and being stigmatized by the mainstream. But margins are created in relationship to a center against which they are compared, a relationship that suggests that the experiences of some can inform a deeper understanding about the lives of all. There are many researchers and writers, including Stephen Hinshaw (2009), Ariel Levy (2005), and Deborah Tolman (2002), who document experiences that fit along the continuum of sexualization among girls in more "mainstream" populations. Their studies are just a few of the many that I include throughout this book to demonstrate the relevance of the continuum of sexualization to the lives of girls and women.

On the continuum, then, one end represents sexualization that occurs as part of girls' day-to-day gender socialization and identity development (Figure 1.1). It is the type of socialization that teaches lessons like the ones Rita described becoming aware of early on. In this book, I will show that this end of the continuum has serious, damaging effects on girls as they grow up to be women in society. The other end of the continuum represents sexual abuses and violence against women and girls, which are severe manifestations of sexual-

Figure 1.1 The Continuum of Sexualization

Socialization/typical ◄─────────────► Sexual abuse/severe

ization. In between these two ends lies everything else that sexualizes girls in contemporary society.

In Rita's case, her studied indifference belies her deeper conflicts. Though the stage performance is superficial, the task of always presenting a readily available sexualized appearance and behavior takes its toll. Even as she admits to "faking it," it seems that to do so drains her, that her identity and self-concept are put on the line in the very effort to appear effortless:

> And it's hard not to get . . . you're acting so intimate—this is hard to explain—you're acting so intimate and physical and you're putting all this energy, to not get something in return is really tough. It's really tough. You put a lot into it. . . . You want to be like, why do I feel I have to do this, I'm the one who got suckered into this, I'm the one who's losing here, I'm losing a piece of me every time I do this. . . . Sometimes I can't bear to look in a guy's eyes while I'm dancing because I'm putting so much of myself into it, I'm afraid they are going to see right through me. And know that I'm faking it. And sometimes I get afraid of that, they're going to see right through me, they're going to know that I'm lying, that this is a big game.

Outline of the Book

The purpose of this book, then, is to examine the "continuum of sexualization." Throughout the years, this concept has shadowed the details of lived experiences that girls and women I've interviewed have described, refusing to go away. In this book, I aim to emphasize particular ways that it is systematically ingrained in girls growing up in the contemporary era, perpetuating limiting identity meanings, at best, and severe damage and destruction, at worst. Book chapters are arranged in a way that I hope most organically allows the continuum of sexualization concept to develop in the minds of readers.

Chapter 2 focuses on gender socialization in today's culture. Such everyday socialization of girls is what constitutes one end of the continuum. This discussion of gender socialization will systematically unfold through the examination of points related to embodiment, "pornified sexualization," and media. Chapter 3, about the processes of sexualization, both fortifies and complicates the main assertions from Chapter 2. It is in Chapter 3 that the continuum of sexualization is presented most comprehensively, clarifying the array of experiences that can exist along the continuum. Not only is there the sexualization that occurs as part of girls' day-to-day gender socialization and identity development, but there is the other end that represents sexual abuses and violence against women and girls. The length of the continuum illustrates the range of experiences that fall between these two ends. It is important to note that Chapter 3 undergirds the framing of the continuum of sexualization as a tool to identify ways in which girls are sexualized (starting at a young age), how this fundamentally incorporates into identity and life for women and girls, and its ultimate effects. It also addresses context, since the continuum of sexualization is located within larger structures of relative privilege or disadvantage. The chapter advances the idea that individuals have a range of experiences in their lives, so for any one girl or woman, sexualization varies as to intensity, duration, and frequency. To fortify these points, I draw extensively on two case study populations—one with a population of women who worked as exotic dancers and one with a population of women who were homeless—and show how contextual factors can exacerbate risks along the continuum. This is a rich addition to a discussion of context, since it is my study of these two populations over the years that crystallized the naming and conceptualization of the continuum of sexualization.

Chapter 4 progresses into the myriad effects the continuum of sexualization can have on women and girls. It traces the extensive personal and social consequences of the continuum. In Chapter 5, the foci of the previous chapters come together in an investigation of pathways that have led to the victimization of girls and women. It is in Chapter 5 that I return to details of the case study populations of exotic dancers and homeless women, looking at how context shaped the effects of their experiences along the continuum of sexualization. In particular, I examine their dreams and goals, decisions, further victimization, and even perpetration as they became adults. Chapter 6 poses some answers to the basic question of how society can stop failing girls and women in the ways the book has detailed. I identify key areas where we do not succeed at protecting girls from risks in society and relate these areas to strategies to counteract such shortcomings. Chapter 7 concludes the book with a challenge to society. In this final chapter, I argue for changes that need to occur at the structural level, with a call to question ideology and social attitudes that perpetuate gender inequality and to bring in programs and services that can affect individual lives. This chapter aims to mobilize readers by relating advocacy for girls to larger social responsibility.

2
Gender Socialization in Today's Culture

Now, I look at stuff like, I can't believe I did that. Now I have a deeper outlook on where that leads you, how society leads you, and how you get sucked into young girls looking the way they look, like sex objects. Even at times I still struggle with that.
—*Tasha, age 23*

Sexualization is part of the gender socialization that girls and women experience. This basic reality undergirds the continuum of sexualization concept, and subsequent chapters will build on related themes and advance it in more detail. First, though, I will make transparent the processes through which sexualization is bundled into the socialization of girls, as well as the complicated ways this is negotiated despite increasingly relentless pressures and ratcheted-up expectations. The groundwork for the continuum is thus laid out in this chapter, beginning with a discussion of gender socialization and moving into the damaging constructs of identity for women and girls.

Gender Socialization

Members of a society learn to behave in conformity with the norms and expectations of that society through a process called socialization. A critically important outcome of the socialization process is the development of a sense of self (Newman 2000). More specifically, one of the basic ways that we develop identity as human beings is through the process of gender socialization—first, discovering that particular body parts translate into a definition of "girl" or "boy," and second, learning through myriad channels, consciously and unconsciously, to act correspondingly "feminine" or "masculine." Though it is bundled with biology, gender is a social construction. Indeed, "gender exists precisely to the extent that biology does not determine the social" (Connell 1995, p. 71). Distinctions between sex and gender are clearly defined in sociology, psychology, and other social science texts and readers (see LaFont 2003; Rothenberg 2007; Yoder 2006) and in existing research (see West and Zimmerman [1987] for a classic article). In essence, sex refers to biological aspects including chromosomes, hormones, and genitals, whereas gender refers to psychologically, socially, and culturally constructed differences between men and women (Yoder 2006). Belknap (2007) adds that "*gender* refers to the ways individuals manage the activities and attitudes prescribed for their sex category" (p. 9; emphasis in original).

In Chapter 3, I will discuss various ways that women in my case studies recalled direct messages about how girls were "supposed" to act. Though it is clear that these are lessons learned via socialization, in dominant discourse they are often conflated with biology, confusing the distinction between gender and sex. The blurring of interpretations contributes to a slippery slope that ascribes a biological essentialism to learned characteristics and behavior. As Tasha, one of the exotic dancers, told me, "I wish I was a guy, because definitely, they don't have to wear makeup, they don't have their period, they don't have to go through labor pains, physically they're stronger, things like that." Though the menstrual cycle and childbearing are biological functions, wearing makeup is certainly not. Instead, makeup is part of the "socialization package"—an achievement of gender in order to look the part. West and Zimmerman (1987) were among the first to identify gender as an "accomplishment" or as something that individuals "do" or "perform" (Butler 1990) through daily behaviors and interactions. Gender is also embodied—it can be "read" via the physical body, both how it is groomed and adorned as well as how it moves through space. Social meanings attributed to bodies signify the appropriate ways to perceive and perform our gendered selves as masculine or feminine. Further, gender transcends daily, individual interactions and embodiment; it is strongly "socially organized" (West & Zimmerman 1987, p. 129). Gender norms generate and continue through organizational structure (Acker 1990) and institutions such as education, media, criminal justice and legal systems, and family, which largely reproduce macrolevel ideologies and power relations. Trying to extract gender from its embeddedness in culture is akin to trying to grab oxygen molecules out of the air with bare hands. Gender is invisible and pervasive, much like what we breathe in and out.

Even before birth, gender expectations are in place for the baby-to-be, and these continue through life. "Girls and boys are taught their society's expectations of appropriate behavior; they grow up to enact their society's gendered social roles" (Lorber 1997, p. 5). Gender socialization begins in earnest when the newborn is declared a boy or girl and correspondingly provided with a blue or pink blanket (Newman 2000). Existing research finds that a child's awareness of gender is already locking in at age two. "By preschool or first grade, children are well aware of their gender, stereotype one another's gender activities, know which parents they are most like, have a thorough knowledge of gender stereotypes, and know the gender of family members and peers" (Chesney-Lind & Irwin 2008, p. 69). Gender performance continues as an ongoing process, and the social imperative to act gender-appropriate pervades all aspects of existence, from behavior, attitude, and comportment to consumption habits, interactions, and everyday and life decisions.

At every developmental stage, an individual is immersed in an environment that includes parents, teachers, media, and peer groups, ensuring the effective installation of gender identity. There are a range of repercussions for any deviation from expected gender norms that serve as social controls that reinforce conformity. I see this around me on a nearly daily basis. As a social scientist, I may admittedly be more attuned to such events than most, but few nearby could avoid hearing the mother at the community pool over the weekend loudly scolding her young boy, who did not want to jump in: "Don't be such a GIRL!" Real men, as most of us have heard, hold revered traits of strength, power, bravery, and emotional stoicism. Attributing femininity to a boy is an insult, an attack that implicitly signifies he is not only less of a man but is also, by being called a girl, of less social value. "In being socialized into the narrow box of what it means to be a 'real man' in this culture, men have to give up aspects of their humanity, their ability to connect intimately with others, and their ability to connect intimately with themselves. . . . And boys know all too well the names, taunts and threats of violence that follow any deviation from this prescription" (Ezzell 2009, p. 11). Gilligan

(1997), known for his research into masculinity and violence, has similar assertions: "Men, much more than women, are taught that to want love or care from others is to be passive, dependent, unaggressive and unambitious or, in short, unmanly; and that they will be subjected to shaming, ridicule and disrespect if they appear unmanly in the eyes of others" (Gilligan 1997, p. 237). These negative responses are powerful mechanisms of social control that reinforce development along the proper gender path.

Why are there such stringent expectations for gender? Why is such a limited range of possibilities acceptable for boys and girls when it comes to this aspect of their identities? The reality is that gender is not simply a benign way to arrange and categorize people. As Morris (2007) similarly points out about race, these are "not just intriguing products of social construction—they are driven by power relations and result in very real patterns of inequality" (p. 411). Interrogations of gender and oppression in Western contemporary society often focus on the concept of patriarchy. Modern feminism critiques patriarchy as an ideology that reduces and degrades women while valuing male dominance in all realms, particularly social, legal, and political ones, and as an ideology in which women's nature is seen to be driven by their biology (Belknap 2007). Gender socialization occurs within this patriarchal context. To further illustrate, Adrienne Rich (1976) provided one of the first comprehensive definitions of the term *patriarchy:*

> A familial-social, ideological, political system in which men—by force, direct pressure, or through ritual, tradition, law, and language, customs, etiquette, education, and the division of labor, determine what part women shall or shall not play, and in which the female is everywhere subsumed under the male. It does not necessarily imply that no woman has power, or that all women in a given culture may not have certain powers. . . . The power of the fathers has been difficult to grasp because it permeates everything, even the language in which we try to describe it. It is diffuse and concrete, symbolic and literal, universal, and expressed with local variations which obscure its universality. (pp. 57–58)

A more contemporary comprehensive definition comes from Ezzell (2009):

> A society is patriarchal to the extent that it is male-dominated, male-identified and male-centered. This doesn't mean that all men

have power over all women or that all men feel powerful in their daily lives. What it means is that men tend to be in positions of power and authority, that what is considered normal and valuable within the culture tends to be associated with men and masculinity, and that the cultural focus of attention tends to be on men and the things that men do. One facet of a patriarchal society, as Johnson notes, is the oppression of women. And one facet of that oppression is men's violence against women. (pp. 8–9)

Identifying patriarchy is useful when problematizing gender constructs, since it is the concept that unveils gender socialization as a nonneutral process. Instead, gender socialization is infused with meanings that maintain a larger system of inequalities, power, and privilege.

Embodiment

Historically, there is a rich literature that examines gender, inequality, and power (see especially Bartky 1990; Bordo 1993; Connell 1990; Kimmel & Messner 2009; Lorber 1998; Messner 2002; Messner & Sabo 1994; Young 1980). What is clear from this wealth of research is that in whatever arena we interrogate gender (e.g., identity, work, sports, body), the different expectations of gender identity for boys and girls are inextricably linked to unequal levels of social value, prestige, or advantage. How do these systems of inequality and privilege get perpetuated through gender socialization? To begin answering this question, consider traditional social constructs of gender identity that typically posit men and women on opposite ends of a spectrum. By examining this polarized arrangement of femininity and masculinity, we start to unpack gender socialization and some of its effects.

The polarized arrangement to which I refer is known as a dualism: "Dualism is the process by which contrasting concepts (for example, masculine and feminine gender identities) are formed by domination and subordination and constructed as oppositional and exclusive" (Plumwood 1993, p. 31). Dualistic constructions such as culture/nature, male/female, and mind/body have existed since the time of ancient Western philosophy. These hierarchical dichotomies undergird the network of assumptions in patriarchal culture. "Female identity in this culture takes shape in relation to a variety of binaries.

A constructing binary of identity (in this case, female identity) is a set of two categories, one marked by relative privilege, the other by relative stigma" (Nagle 1997, p. 5). As with the young boy who did not want to jump in the pool, Dines (2010) finds that "to be 'unmanly' is, of course, within our gender binary system, to be feminine, and here lies the essence of gender socialization for males: they need, at all times, to distance themselves as much as possible from anything constructed by the culture as feminine" (p. 60). A feminist assessment reveals that within dualistic thought, women are reduced to the body and associated with nature; women are "embodied and inferior on the basis of that embodiment" (Olsen 1996, p. 212). Men are portrayed as disembodied—or if they have bodies, these bodies are incidental and unproblematic. In contrast, women's bodies are messy, uncontained, uncontrolled (Lee 1998; Lorber 1997; Olsen 1996). "The supposedly normal body for a long time was that of a middle-class, young adult white man. Female physiology, including menstruation, pregnancy, and menopause, became pathology" (Lorber 1997, p. 51).

The framing of female embodiment as pathological is not historical artifact. Paula, one of the dancers I interviewed, used the process of menstruation to "explain" why women cannot be trusted:

> And women are very vindictive. Never trust anything [*sic*] who bleeds without being cut. Women are evil, period. I am too. Outside the club environment I have limited interaction with women, because I know how they are. Don't trust something that bleeds without being cut. And not only that, but they do it for seven days and don't die.

Paula uses a biological process to explain why women are "evil." I was initially thrown off when I listened to Paula say this; though I had heard it before, I did not expect it from her. My first thought was that projecting evil and untrustworthy connotations onto women's biology supports Paula's position as a competitor for dollars in an environment where everything is focused on women's bodies. Paula activates an age-old strategy that discredits women based on their embodiment. But why would Paula say something that is so easily turned back on her? She even identifies herself as "evil," which seems self-alienating, if not self-hating. Schaffner (2006), in her research with girls in juvenile detention centers, points out the emerging trend found in the scholarship about at-risk populations of girls hating or mistrusting other girls. Girls who grow up amid multiple oppressions, especially those who have been victimized and endured childhood traumas, who see women in their lives regularly devalued, and who absorb misogyny "from the larger culture, particularly when they witness women being treated less respectfully and as if they were less important than men" (p. 142) are more often divided from other girls and increasingly "male identified." It would not be difficult to pinpoint contexts that shape Paula's anger. Her father was abusive. She was neglected, left in the care of a 4-year-old brother while she was still an infant. By her account, she went to twenty-seven different foster homes. Now 19 years old, she "raised herself." It may be that these misogynist, essentialist statements are a way of claiming agency in a world where she has been completely powerless to control events in her life. She describes "shoving a spike" from her heel into a man's temple after he violated her during one of her stage performances. In such a context, as Schaffner (2006) notes of the violence committed by girls in her study, "girls' aggression is seen as a real response to real problems. The girls' accounts . . . showed their violence to be an expression of an imbibed misogyny and a way of attempting to fight back—as a power of the powerless" (p. 145). This helps contextualize the disturbing attributions to women made by Paula.

The construction of female bodies as aberrant has a long history: Foucault (1988a) notes that in the seventeenth century, women's bodies were seen as "penetrable" and "porous," and the "entire female body is riddled by obscure but strangely direct paths of sympathy . . . it encloses a perpetual possibility of hysteria" (p. 154). The hysterization and pathologization of the female body correlates with assumptions of irrationality and emotionality. Again, then, the implications of the "slippery slope" of biological essentialism come to the surface. Charles Darwin's theory of evolution promoted the argument that women use the majority of their energies on biological reproduction and so have little energy remaining for mental or physical growth (Weitz 1998). There have been real implications of these gender constructs: "This schema worked to justify the exclusion of women from the domains of the academy, of science, and from generally being accorded epistemic authority and even credibility, because women were well known to be much more subject to bodily distractions, hormonal cycles, emotional disturbances and the like" (Alcoff 1996, p. 16). As Martin (1992) states, "it is no accident that 'natural' facts about women, in the form of claims about biology, are often used to justify social stratification based on gender" (p. 17).

Sexualization

A related and central aspect of gender socialization and "emphasized embodiment" for girls is sexualization. A major facet of sexualization is sexual objectification, which occurs "when a woman's sexual parts or sexual functions are separated out from her person, reduced to the status of mere instruments, or else regarded as if they were capable of representing her" (Bartky 1990, p. 35). Modern feminist thought advances the belief that within patriarchal culture, the female body is reduced to particular meanings like that of sexual object (see Bartky 1990; Bordo 1993; Chapkis 1986; Griffin 1981; Martin 1992). According to the *Report of the APA Task Force on the Sexualization of Girls* (APA 2007), there are several aspects to sexualization, and these distinguish it from healthy sexuality. Any one of the four components is indicative of sexualization:

1. A person's value comes only from his or her sexual appeal or behavior, to the exclusion of other characteristics.
2. A person is held to a standard that equates physical attractiveness (narrowly defined) with being sexy.
3. A person is sexually objectified—that is, made into a thing for others' sexual use, rather than seen as a person with the capacity for independent action and decisionmaking.
4. Sexuality is inappropriately imposed upon a person (i.e., on a child). (APA 2007, p. 1)

As girls grow up, the cultural overemphasis on their sexualized bodies becomes increasingly integrated into female identity. "This highly disciplined body has now become the key site where gender is enacted and displayed on a daily basis. To be feminine requires not only the accoutrements of hypersexuality—high heels, tight clothes, and so on—but also a body that adheres to an extremely strict set of standards" (Dines 2010, pp. 109–110). It is often this view of female bodies that garners women the most attention (Bartky 1990; Chapkis 1986), though the sexy ideal is largely unattainable despite the time, effort, energy, and money many women devote in service to its achievement:

> The disciplinary project of femininity is a "setup": it requires such radical and extensive measures of bodily transformation that virtually every woman who gives herself to it is destined in some degree to fail. Thus, a measure of shame is added to a woman's sense that the body she inhabits is deficient. . . . In spite of unrelenting pres-

sure to "make the most of what they have," women are ridiculed and dismissed for the triviality of their interest in such "trivial" things as clothes and make-up. Further, the narrow identification of woman with sexuality and the body in a society that has for centuries displayed profound suspicion toward both does little to raise her status. (Bartky 1990, p. 72)

As part of gender socialization, then, girls learn the "value" of their sexualization. They learn that emphasizing their sexualized appearance is important, that being sexy gets attention and might even garner some favoritism or rewards, as Rita described at the start of Chapter 1.

There are few spaces in which gender performance is as obvious as in the strip club, where women are paid to embody the sexualized image. Like all women, those who work as exotic dancers learn early on of the contemporary ideal of feminine attractiveness. The club environment, however, also strips away pretense, promoting the straightforward exchange of female sexualized body for cash. Women's livelihood in this environment depends on how successfully they portray and enact the image. Pressure to meet the ideal is reinforced in many ways in the club beyond the customer's wallet. For example, one club manager, Joe, discussed on a radio program that I listened to how he ran a purportedly "upscale gentleman's club." According to several women I interviewed who worked at his club, he forced them to "weigh-in" and meet his arbitrary weight standards or risk being fired. He even directed them to drugs to help them lose weight:

> So I remember one time, Joe came in and was like, "Ok, all you fat girls are weighing in. Including you." And I'm like, I'm thick, I'm black, I'm supposed to be big. He's like, "No, including you. You guys are all weighing in." And he told you, "Lose five, or lose ten. This is how much time you have. Lose six." This was also his way of weeding out girls. That's how I got into crystal [methamphetamine]. I'm all, how am I supposed to lose ten pounds in two weeks? He goes, "Why don't you talk to so-and-so?" So I talked to so-and-so and she offered me crystal. She gave me crystal, and that's how it started. That was my weight-loss drug. (Valerie)

Joe's not-so-subtle directive leads to substance abuse and addiction as a weight-control mechanism. As Julie told me, "Soon as I stopped doing crystal, girl, I gained 30 pounds. Now I do everything in the world to stay fit, but it's just not the same as that 'magical' diet." Irene, another dancer, had liposuction, although she "did not need the liposuction. I think I weighed 125 pounds. But I was so obsessed with being skinny for the job." It has been suggested that eating disorders such as anorexia and bulimia may be related to the objectification of women and the perception of thinness as ideal female beauty (McLorg & Taub 1987). This is only exacerbated in a context in which club personnel monitor the women's weight and customers financially reward them for being thin. So in addition to drugs and cosmetic surgery, the women also described eating disorders, laxatives, and obsessive exercising as techniques to stay skinny enough to meet (management/customer/societal) standards.

> I wish I was a lot skinnier. I eat once a day. Before that, when I first started [dancing], I was on laxatives. I would eat whatever I wanted, but I'd take laxatives, and the doctor told me I had to stop. I would take laxatives to where it would mess up your body. Now I eat once a day, and it's really fine for me that way. Sometimes I wish I didn't have to eat at all. . . . I don't go throw up, I've never had that problem. I just don't eat. (Samantha)

The dancers were also hyperaware of how they measured up against other workers and critiqued their own bodies even more harshly. One example is Marie's recollection: "You have guys give you money and say, if you had [big] boobs, you'd have the perfect body. And you hear those things all the time." Gina stated:

> When I was performing I was constantly comparing myself to other people. Constantly. 'Cause there's always somebody who looks better. There's always somebody who's got a tighter body, bigger boobs, who's got better looking abs. . . . You become very in tune with how you look and who is making money and how they look. And you know, most of the girls who are making money have dyed blonde hair, and big boobs, and they look like Barbie dolls. . . . It really affected me personally when I would walk up to a guy and he would look me up and down and say, no thanks. . . . I would start feeling down on myself, what's wrong with me, my boobs aren't big enough, my hair's not blonde enough, I'm not tall enough, I'm not thin enough. . . . I'd start picking apart my body. I'd sit in the dress-

ing room, wondering: what can I change about myself, to make myself more appealing to these guys?

Jessie, who is Mexican American, felt that she was lacking in relation to other women in the club on a number of levels: "And I'm really self-conscious about my body, because I have three kids. . . . And I'd see all these girls, pretty girls, white girls, flat stomach, boob jobs, and I'm like, oh my gosh." Jessie's quote included skin color as a component of her idealized assessment of physical beauty; she incorporated "whiteness" into her concept of what she lacks in appeal. This invokes cultural constructions of feminine beauty as white, and the exclusion or distortion of nonwhite bodies within this context (hooks 1997). Jessie's inclusion of "white" along with "pretty," "flat stomachs," and "boob jobs" also reflects a construction of whiteness as an aspect of the physical self that can be constructed to more closely approximate the ideal. In her discussion of Tina Turner, bell hooks (1997) notes that the racist aesthetic of "blonde hair as the epitome of beauty" is often reinforced through the use of wigs and other artificial means, reproducing whiteness as the standard of feminine attractiveness.

Comportment and posture are additional ways of successfully performing sexualized embodiment. Rita described, "We're not posing naturally. You don't [normally] stick your butt out or your chest out that far, and suck in. But somewhat, but when I dance, out of habit now my body just goes to the shape I want it to be in, and I have my own routine that I go through." There are seemingly endless mechanisms of maintenance in service to the sexualized image. Even a hairless pubic area is regulation in a club that, according to one interviewee, had a sign posted in the dressing room: "Girls are getting too hairy!" While menstruating, some described the practice of "cut and tuck"—after inserting a tampon the string is cut and tucked inside the vagina so as to be invisible outside the body. The irony here is that the "real," unavoidable biologic aspects of being a woman are hidden and minimized while the "pretend" or manufactured aspects are foregrounded. Embodied, sexualized gender performance trumps reality, which makes the artificiality of social constructs imposed on girls and women all the more clear.

I could see for myself the stark contrast of reality to artificiality when I spent time with some of the women like Skye, who has breast implants, dyes her hair blonde, has a deep tan, and wears blue contacts in her brown eyes. The original parts of Skye slip through cracks in the facade. From across the table, as we have lunch together, I notice traces of brown that are visible behind her blue iris. The darker roots of her platinum color are evident at the scalp. Her skin tone takes on a neon-orange hue. Another young woman, Cory, tells me how at 21 she has already had extensive cosmetic surgery, including hair implants, nose job, cheek implants, chin surgery, breast implants, tummy tuck, and liposuction, costing a grand total of about $30,000. Once informed by her doctor that she had gotten breast cancer from her huge implants, however, they consequently had to be removed. Her main worry was about the appearance of her breasts rather than her health. "I was pissed. . . . Basically, I didn't care about the cancer. I care about me not having big boobs. And then once you get a boob job all that skin is stretched. So it was going to go back and it was going to be saggy." Samantha, who has had two nose surgeries and two "boob jobs," had a response not unlike Cory's. "I got in a car accident, and when I was in the car I never thought about death. All I thought about was, oh my god, I hope nothing happens to my face. I really think if anything ever happens to my face, my body, I would kill myself. This is me, this is all I have. I wouldn't be able to go on with my life." The dramatic statement that "this is me, this is all I have" might speak to the reliance on appearance for livelihood. But it also suggests that this sexualization, though artificial, runs deeper than superficial appearance. Boundaries between identity and performance have blurred; it is hard to separate the two.

In general, sexualization is not a neutral aspect of gender socialization for girls, but in fact plugs directly into systemic inequalities. One explanation is derived from French feminists such as Irigaray (1985a, 1985b) and Cixous and Clement (1986), who describe modern patriarchy as "phallocentric." Within a phallocentric culture, they argue, women have little control in legitimate arenas of power. They do not dominate the shaping of laws, language, or the development of thought; they are excluded from political, social, and economic realms that create and perpetuate power relations. Deprived of these types of power in a phallocentric society, Irigaray (1985a) noted that women engage the market in one of the few ways to which they have access: by using the sexualized body as a commodity or item of exchange. Yet this does not truly appropriate legitimate power or grant women the structural leverage to affect change, largely because it does not elevate women's status to equal competitors in a market that exploits them:

> Women today are still held captive by images that ultimately tell lies about women. The biggest lie is that conforming to this hypersexualized image will give women real power in the world, since in a porn culture, our power rests, we are told, not in our ability to shape the institutions that determine our life chances but in having a hot body that men desire and women envy. (Dines 2010, p. 102)

Relentless pursuit of the sexualized image maintains women's diminished status as objects. As I have stated elsewhere:

> As they mature, all girls learn of the significance of their sexualized bodies. They find that their bodies are often the focus of male attention. They may also find that the value of their sexual parts is sometimes thought to eclipse other aspects of their identities, such as their intelligence, ambition, fortitude, or humor. In addition, the feeling of power attained when the sexualized body can be used to get attention from, distract or manipulate men hardly compares to men's power in social, political, economic or cultural realms. Yet the micro-level rewards that women do receive for their sexualized bodies often reinforce the feminine preoccupation with sexualized appearance. (Wesely 2002, p. 1204)

Gender expectations are fluidly folded into identity development as children grow up. Since gender socialization maintains and reinforces dominant constructions of power and inequality, these too become internalized by the individual. Foucault's (1990, 1995) work facilitates an understanding of this process. In *Discipline and Punish* (1995), Foucault traces historically how power moved from a central source (i.e., the sovereign) and became disseminated in diffuse and multiple ways, normalized into all areas of life as a means of regulating and reproducing subjects. He compares decentralized or "disciplinary" power to Jeremy Bentham's Panopticon, a model prison in which the inmates feel hypervisible and so become self-regulating or disciplining (pp. 200–201). In contrast to central power, panoptical surveillance exists "in the bodies that can be individualized" (p. 208). Foucault's concept of the "docile body" is (self) disciplined in accordance with dominant power relations; it both represents power in society and manifests it through daily practice and performance. A feminist criticism of Foucault is that he rarely addresses women directly in his work and excludes the lived body experiences of women in his analysis (Bartky 1990; Diamond & Quinby 1988; Lydon 1988; Martin 1992), which risks voiding the specificity of gendered inequalities. Foucault's discussion of normalized power similarly falls short of an interrogation of gendered power and its relationship to women's embodiment. Diamond and Quinby (1988) point out that Foucault uses men's writings in his work but ignores feminist research about the body. Martin (1992) takes umbrage with Foucault's assertion of a "slackening of the hold on the body" (Foucault 1995, p. 10) as the era of physical punishment ended. She argues that women "suffer the alienation of parts of the self much more acutely than men. For one thing, becoming sexually female entails inner fragmentation of the self. A woman must become only a physical body in order to be sexual" (Martin 1992, p. 21).

Despite these criticisms, feminist scholars have found ways to integrate Foucault's work into their analyses. Bartky (1990) integrates Foucault's concepts of power, discipline, and the body, claiming that women "discipline" their bodies in the name of (hetero)sexualized beauty and that this maintains patriarchal power over women. Women have historically shaped, molded, covered, painted, cut, and otherwise artificially altered their bodies in order to conform to gendered expectations, and Bartky (1990) links feminine body discipline to Foucaultian concepts of panoptical power. She states, "In contemporary patriarchal culture, a panoptical male connoisseur resides within the consciousness of most women" (1990, p. 34); or, as Dines (2010) puts it: "Women have so internalized the male gaze that they have now become their own worst critics" (p. 110). Women's practices in service to femininity can be interpreted as self-regulating disciplines of the docile body that reinforce the status quo of power. Panoptical surveillance results in a gaze directed inward, a type of self-objectification. Foucault speaks of "recognition by mirror" (1988a), in which the individual (in his description, the madman), is forced to see "himself" as object. In Foucault's interpretation of the mirror, the objectification of the self allows the madman to see that he is, objectively, mad. In a state of perpetual judgment, the madman is continually reminded of his objective self. "By this play of mirrors, as by silence, madness is ceaselessly called upon to judge itself. But beyond this, it is at every moment judged from without; judged not by moral or scientific conscience, but by a sort of invisible tribunal in permanent session" (Foucault 1988a, p. 265). For the woman, the invisible tribunal becomes her own gaze upon herself.

Complicating Gender Identity

Thus far, this chapter has focused on deconstructing gender socialization and unearthing its links to larger structural inequalities. As Lorber (1998) notes, "Analyzing the social processes that construct the categories we call 'female and male,' 'women and men,' and 'homosexual and heterosexual' uncovers the ideology and power differentials congealed in these categories" (p. 13). Yet it is important before proceeding further to complicate straightforward, static concepts of gender identity. A postmodern analysis challenges the framing of individuals as passive recipients of gender meanings. Postmodernism is characterized by fragmented and fractured identities (Harvey 1989) and resists the notion of any one established reality or truth. One critique of postmodernism is that by rendering identities and meanings fluid, it dilutes the import and impact of social inequalities. More comprehensive is a postmodern feminist approach, which examines both the day-to-day, lived experiences of women and the ways that gender oppression may intersect with these experiences. An application of postmodern feminism to constructs of gender identity is to conceptualize gender as performance, rather than as something inherently part of the individual. Foregrounding the ways we "do gender" (West & Zimmerman 1987) reveals the artificiality and partiality of gender constructs. When individuals "do gender," they make efforts to display or perform their gendered selves in a particular way. When this is repeated over time, it begins to appear natural. Butler (1990) notes that gender requires a performance that is consistently repeated through regulatory practices. "There is no gender identity behind the expressions of gender; that identity is performatively constituted by the very 'expressions' that are said to be its results" (p. 25). As something that is done or performed, gender then seems to parody or mock the idea of original gender; it becomes an act without origin.

Beginning with the second volume of *The History of Sexuality* (1985), Foucault complicates notions of bodies as docile, passive recipients of discipline and focuses on individual agency in creating and re-creating the self. Foucault (1988b) suggests that "technologies of the self" are mechanisms through which individuals create, transform, and understand themselves. This expands his original and more unilateral assessments of docile bodies and is a rich addition to feminist concepts of gender identity and the body. To argue that individuals do not just passively reproduce power through disciplinary practices but also play an active role in negotiating their identities deepens our understanding of how women's bodily practices are an ongoing process of identity transformation.

Given these postmodern feminist and Foucaultian theories, it seems that opportunities exist to challenge and resist rigid gender norms. In other work (Wesely 2003), I have discussed "body technologies," which are the techniques we engage to change or alter our physical appearance, temporarily or permanently. Scholarship about particular body technologies such as cosmetic surgery (Balsamo 1997; Dull & West 1991; Kaw 1998; Morgan 1998) and bodybuilding (Balsamo 1997; Heywood 1997; Holmlund 1997; Wesely 2001) has pointed out the ways that body technologies can both reinforce and challenge "natural" conceptions of gender. For instance, sex performer Annie Sprinkle blurs boundaries between performance and porn; she parodies pornographic images of her body by revealing its artificial construction. In an image called *Anatomy of a Pinup Photo,* Sprinkle is pictured as a porn star but labels in writing on the photo each body technology, providing helpful statements such as "Mandatory fake beauty mark/Breasts are real but sag. Bra lifts breasts/Hemorrhoids don't show, thank goodness/Gloves cover tattoos for a more All-American girl effect, borrowed from Antoinette/ I can't walk and can barely hobble/Corset hides a very big belly" (Williams 1997, p. 373) and so on. By systematically noting the body technologies she uses, Sprinkle unveils the performativity of her sexually objectified body.

The exotic dancers I interviewed, though clearly a population who construct and perform the body in a hypersexualized image, also felt they engaged and presented their physical selves beyond such one-dimensional meanings. They wanted to make money, but they also wanted to feel unique, special, and different. "Women's active choices about their bodies and identities might be constrained by the contexts in which they participate," however (Wesely 2003, p. 647). In the strip club, a certain look reaps the largest financial reward. How to assert uniqueness without losing appeal to customers? This is difficult. Rita described technologies such as tattoos or piercings as ways of making a dancer appear—and feel—different or unusual.

There's only so many things you can do to be interesting. That's why girls get tattoos or get pierced. You're standing there [naked] in shoes, what can you do? We all look the same. You've seen one pair [of breasts], you've seen them all. You try to be different, you think, oh, it's going to be my tan or my makeup or my clothes. I hate that.

Rita was frustrated by the failure of particular body technologies—her "tan," "makeup," or "clothes"—to truly differentiate her from the other dancers. She found that tattoos and piercings were engaged by dancers to counter this failing. Body technologies used to achieve the sexualized look may unfortunately have the effect of neutralizing individuality, rather than serving as a means of its expression. The disproportionate focus on embodied appearance in the strip club was, at times, empty and unsatisfying. This is especially evident in a statement made by Angel: "I kind of got bored with my body. . . . I would get dry runs on my body. Which are when they give you a tattoo without any ink. I had it done in different spots just to see what it feels like."

Clearly, individuals struggle with identity meanings that are limited by the gender socialization directive and the power inequalities inherent within it, the social contexts within which they act, and the resources available to them. Further, I propose that there are new, alarming strictures around gender expectations that are challenging the abilities of girls and women to generate healthier identities for themselves.

The Media and Pornified Sexualization

It gets to the point, is there anywhere I can go [without being ogled or hit on]. . . . I don't think men have that problem. If I wasn't a woman. You see a good-looking guy in the store, and you're not going to walk up to him and say, nice tomatoes you're picking out there! I feel like I can't go anywhere. I would definitely say society sets it up that way. You don't see a lot of men all over magazine covers. You see women all over. And billboards, what have you. It's almost like it gives men permission to treat women like [objects] . . . if you see any kind of woman walking down the street, it's like it gives them permission just because she's a woman. (Marie)

We live in an "image-based culture," defined as one in which images dominate other forms of communication, including the spoken and written word (Dines 2009). Within this environment, advertising and media portray images of girls as mature sexual objects at younger and younger ages; in contrast, sexualized images of adult women often appear childlike or "infantilized" (think of adult women in "schoolgirl" outfits, pigtails, or licking lollipops; pop artist Christina Aguilera demonstrated all three in a Sketchers "naughty and nice" ad) (Bartky 1990; Bass & Thornton 1991; Kilbourne 1987, 2000, 2010). The *Report of the APA Task Force on the Sexualization of Girls* (APA 2007) names this "age compression" and calls for more research exploration of the "'adultification' of young girls and 'youthification' of adult women" (p. 5). The *Report of the APA Task Force* also points out that "anyone (girls, boys, men, women) can be sexualized. But when children are imbued with adult sexuality, it is often imposed upon them rather than chosen by them" (APA 2007, p. 1). Indeed, one of the many problems with these sorts of constructions is that they present a "distorted version of children's sexuality and their alleged capacity for seductiveness" (Davis 1999, p. 95). When sexualization blurs the line between child and adult, the child looks sexual, and this "is a very dangerous thing to do because it arouses sexual interest. Because the child looks this way, the reasoning becomes that being sexual with her is not so bad" (Sharon Boles as cited in Davis 1999, p. 115). This slippery slope is what ultimately leads to severe consequences for girls in the form of exploitation and abuse, a topic that will be explored in later chapters.

There are innumerable examples of music and video idols who portray such images and are emulated and imitated by children and adolescents. One such example is former teen sensation Britney Spears. Moving from child beauty pageants to the Mickey Mouse Club, Spears then became a star who, in her late teens, blurred the line between pop and porn in her sexualized performances, starting with the music video to "Baby One More Time." She begins her on-screen gyrations in a revealing schoolgirl uniform, complete with micromini and bared midriff, her hair in braided pigtails and her mouth outlined in heavy lipstick. Obviously, the juxtaposition of the sex-simulated dance choreography and adult makeup with a little girl's (hacked off) uniform and hairdo is no accident and certainly not the first of its kind to be broadcast. This is a stylized, packaged image, but one that nonetheless reminds us how frequently we dangerously tread on the boundaries between women and child. Farley (2009) notes, "At the age of 17, [Britney Spears] became the middle age man's fantasy of the school girl who is secretly a slut" (p. 148). Further blurring the line between pop girl and porn star, Spears later went on to employ long-time porn director Gregory Dark to direct her videos.

It is frightening to see the new developments that build on this type of sexualization. Constantly bombarded by images of the young, sexualized female body in advertisements, movies, and television, the average consumer's attention is maintained only by an amping up of these images. "This has led to an increasingly pornographic media landscape in which the codes and conventions that inform pornography filter down to mainstream imagery to such a degree that the images we now see in mainstream media are almost on a par with those that were found in soft-core porn just a decade ago" (Dines 2009, p. 122). A bird's-eye view of the mainstreaming of porn reveals everything ranging from T-shirts that tout "Porn Star" (and are worn by twelve-year-olds) to "pole-dancing" fitness classes (I just noticed one advertised in my neighborhood yesterday). In fact, "pole-dancing toys were marketed to 4- and 5-year-olds by Tesco, the largest chain in the United Kingdom. . . . Other prostitution-themed items sold by Tesco included T-shirts for 6-year-old girls with the words 'so many boys, so little time'" (Farley 2009, p. 152). Hinshaw (2009) notes that in 2003, $1.6 million worth of thong underwear was purchased for girls aged 7 to 12. This pornified expectation becomes part of a young girl's identity and self-worth along with the social construction of her as a female. Levy (2005) calls this "raunch" culture and defines it as "a tawdry, tarty, cartoon-like version of female sexuality" (p. 5), a "porny" image of girls that is relentlessly marketed through the fashion industry. A term has been applied to the youngest girls being targeted by marketing and then buying (into) this image: *prosti-tots* (Hinshaw 2009, p. 110). In her book *Pornland: How Porn Has Hijacked Our Sexuality,* Dines (2010) acknowledges that although the fashion industry has always sexualized girls, the difference now is the way that this "look" is inspired by the sex industry:

> The low-slung jeans, the short skirt that rides up our legs as we sit down, the thong, the tattoo on the lower back, the pierced belly button, the low-cut top that shows cleavage, the high heels that contort our calves, and the pouting glossed lips all conspire to make us look like a bargain-basement version of the real thing. . . . The magazines that instruct us in the latest "must-have" fashions have no

shortage of ads that depict, in excruciating detail, what it means to be feminine in today's porn culture. (p. 103)

Despite hopes for alternatives to this image for girls, the possibilities appear to decrease rather than open up over time, since the level to which the pornified sexual image has saturated the market starts to crowd out other options. The media have been directly implicated in creating this environment for girls, though they are not the only influence. "Education, the family, and other modes of disseminating rules and norms function to shape and discipline girls' experiences of and knowledge about gender" (Driscoll 2002, p. 129), as do adolescent subcultures and peer groups (see Chesney-Lind & Irwin 2008) and girls' interpersonal relationships. These relationships can include parents, teachers, and peers. For instance, parents can overemphasize to girls the importance of attractiveness as a goal. Among peer groups, "both male and female peers have been found to contribute to the sexualization of girls—girls by policing each other to ensure conformance with standards of thinness and sexiness . . . and boys by sexually objectifying and harassing girls" (APA 2007).

Still, the media remain an institution that serves as reflection and reinforcement of social norms and an aspect of culture that reifies dominant power relations and the status quo (Ezzell 2009). Most researchers agree that the "media [are] among the most important agents of socialization influencing American teens and young adults" (CASA 2003, p. 69), and media effects are pervasive and far-reaching. There are innumerable facets to the mass media's insidious grasp, and one reason the grasp is so strong is its ubiquity. Not only do children and teens have access to the content through myriad venues, but there is nearly limitless availability.

> These days, children's exposure to screen media extends way beyond television or film. MP3 players, cell phones, and personalized DVD players all display media content targeted at children. Children are subject to screens at home, in restaurants, at school, in their pediatrician's waiting room, in the back seats of mini-vans, in airplanes, and even on supermarket shopping carts. . . . In addition, the plethora of media-linked toys—including video and online games based on movies and TV shows—that dominate the market is another commercial phenomenon inhibiting creative play and locking children into rigidly prescribed versions of how men and women behave. (Linn 2009, p. 35)

On average, children ages 2–18 watch about forty hours of television a week after school (Linn 2009), and prime-time shows alone are loaded with images that sexualize and degrade women (Maine 2009). Further, teens spend between four and five hours a day listening to music and watching music videos (such as those on MTV). Youth from 12- to 20-years-old purchase 26 percent of all movie tickets in a year, though they make up only 16 percent of the population (CASA 2003). Reports that examined a range of media from video games to magazines find that "sexist media" enables men's violence against women and constrains the gender expectations for both boys and girls. A study of gender and hypersexuality in the 300 top-grossing G, PG, or PG-13 films between 1990 and 2006 revealed several key findings: seventy-three percent of the speaking roles were male, the female characters were either hypersexualized or homemakers, and females were more than five times as likely to be in sexually revealing outfits (Maine 2009). Dietz (1998) addressed gender roles in video games, finding that female characters were most likely to appear as victims or sex objects. Violent video games such as Grand Theft Auto are well known for promoting gendered violence, such as the "opportunity" to rape or kill a simulated woman (Dines 2010). Further, popular television shows and films generate an inundation of merchandising with toys, dolls, figurines, posters, furniture and decor, school supplies, accessories, clothing, Internet games, and interactive networking sites that are rigorously foisted upon youth everywhere they turn, often through the same channels that popularized the media item in the first place.

For instance, Disney secures the loyalty of children and teens through "an endless loop of toys, clothing, food, accessories and media" that ensures that "little girls buy into a lifestyle rooted in all things Disney sells" (Linn 2009, p. 41). When girls buy into Disney, however, they are locking onto something shown to have an adverse effect on their healthy gender development. In his book *Fugitive Cultures: Race, Violence, and Youth,* Giroux (1996) points out that Disney is far from free of the dynamics of ideology, politics, and power:

> The boundaries between entertainment, education and commercialization collapse through the sheer omnipotence of Disney's reach into diverse spheres of life. . . . Even more disturbing is the widespread belief that Disney's trademarked innocence renders it unac-

countable for the diverse ways in which it shapes the sense of reality it provides for children as they take up specific and often sanitized notions of identity. (p. 94)

Specifically, Giroux (1996) argues that Disney's female characters fall within rigid gender roles, are "ultimately subordinate to males, and define their sense of power and desire almost exclusively in terms of dominant male narratives" (p. 101). Both gender stereotyping and embodied imagery are perpetuated here (for instance, Giroux describes Ariel in the animated film *The Little Mermaid* as a "slightly anorexic Barbie doll"). Disney's ideological paradigm includes implications associated with a long history of racism evident throughout studio productions and racial stereotyping in contemporary portrayals and imagery. Giroux (1996) provides excellent, detailed references that substantiate the race and class constructions perpetuated by Disney. "Issues regarding the construction of gender, race, class, caste, and other aspects of self and collective identity are defining principles of Disney's films for children" (p. 109). And still, the Disney empire is one of three multinational corporations controlling most of children's commercial culture. It is no longer simply a fairy tale that children can creatively consider, but a commodified packaging of culture that promotes specific constructs and norms. Disney thus serves as an excellent exemplar of the sweeping and insidious nature of media influence.

Linn (2009) asserts that the manner in which the market is dominated by stereotyped gender roles and unrealistic body types promoted by brands like Disney (among others) contributes to a commercially constructed phenomenon that deprives children of middle childhood. Stages of development identify these "preadolescent" girls as 8 to 11 years old. At this point girls are relatively stable physically, not "grappling with great hormonal surges and unwieldy body changes. It's a time when children don't have to worry about their bodies and are able to form friendships with members of the opposite sex without having to worry about sexual overtones" (Linn 2009, p. 48). At this age girls tend to be strong, self-confident, and outspoken. A term has been ascribed to the preadolescent or middle childhood group who are typically still in elementary school: *tweens*. Again, this group of girls is not yet developmentally affected by teen angst and is able to have nonnuanced opposite-sex relationships. "They engage in activities that interest them without much concern for the gender-appropriateness of those activities" (CASA 2003, p. 13). It is in "early adolescence" (middle-school age) when girls start to show signs of physical development, may feel awkward about their bodies, evidence concerns about physical and sexual attractiveness, and struggle with identity. "Middle adolescence" is typically designated as high-school age, when girls become extremely preoccupied with appearance and their bodies and sexual attractiveness. At this stage of adolescence, girls have frequently changing relationships but still put great emphasis on their peer groups while withdrawing emotionally from parents. Finally, in "later adolescence" and then in "early adulthood" (post–high school age), when girls have a more cohesive sense of identity and increased independence, peer relationships take an appropriate place while conflicts with parents tend to decrease (CASA 2003).

It is the most developmentally unencumbered group of girls, the preadolescent tweens, who have in recent years become an industry-targeted consumer demographic. Specific items promoted to them range from "cell phones to thong underpants" (Linn 2009, p. 45). Though tweens are treated as teen consumers and may quickly learn to navigate new technological gadgets, this behavior belies their developmental limitations in processing the adult content they receive. For instance, they are not equipped to analyze the objectification of themselves in the rigid, stereotyped images they see promoted in the media (Farley 2009) or to think about it critically. The unexamined attitudes instilled by these sources and products are toxic, and yet they are the ones that become ingrained in the psychological makeup of children. This is especially true for the pornified, sexualized images so seamlessly included in daily media exposure:

> However, today's children are bombarded with large doses of graphic sexual content that they cannot process and that are often frightening. When children struggle to make sense of mature sexual content, they are robbed of valuable time for age-appropriate developmental tasks. They may also begin to engage in precocious sexual behavior and learn lessons that will undermine their ability to have healthy, caring relationships in which sex plays a part when they are older. (Levin 2009, p. 84)

As a multi-billion-dollar industry with huge influence on children and adolescents, the effects of the media and their pornified sexualization of girls should not be underestimated. "Teens are keenly aware of cultural standards and ideals through intense exposure to the media and its messages in all forms . . . as a result media exerts an immense psychological impact on them" (Maine 2009, p. 71). The significance of having such limited images available within a boundless industry is that girls are left with little to go on if they want to form a more multidimensional identity. And as Dines (2010) points out, to be seen not reflecting the image promoted by the mainstream is tantamount to being invisible altogether. At a time when fitting in is so important, being invisible is a nearly untenable option.

It is not surprising that adolescent girls struggle with what it means to become a sexual being when this aspect of their identities is paradoxically emphasized and caricatured while also trivialized and degraded. Somehow, girls must negotiate these conflicting meanings. Chesney-Lind and Irwin (2008) point out that less is known about the period of gender socialization that occurs during girls' adolescence. What is known from the literature, however, is that parents are talking to their teen girls about "maturity," "commitment," and "real love" and not about their daughter's sexuality. At the same time, girls are focusing more on feedback from peer groups and attention from boys (Chesney-Lind & Irwin 2008). "According to the sociologists and anthropologists whose accounts of culture and society became newly visible in the twentieth century, girls' sexual selves have the most pervasive effects on their social lives and determine much of the difficulty of feminine adolescence" (Driscoll 2002, p. 154). Driscoll's statement suggests that a better system of helping adolescent girls through the growth of new aspects of identity might alleviate some of the "difficulty" of feminine adolescence—yet our culture seems to have lost its grip on how to properly guide girls as they become mature sexual beings. School systems are typically restrictive regarding sexual education, with some not permitting it at all (Farley 2009). In the three decades through the years of the George W. Bush administration, not one federally funded program on comprehensive sex education existed, though the country has spent nearly $1 billion on abstinence education since 1996 (Levy 2005). Driscoll (2002) calls this a "disjunction between sexual maturity and sex education" (p. 154). When we deny children access to meaningful information about their sexual development, they learn from the sources available to them. "In the absence of comprehensive and timely discussions about sex between children and their parents, adolescents are largely getting their sex education and socialization through the media" (Ezzell

2009, p. 10). Girls and boys consume a steady diet of media images as their main source of education about what it means to grow up female or male in our society.

In fact, the pornified sexualized image of women appears to have grown in nearly inverse proportion to the useful information provided to youth about sex and sexuality. Levy (2005) points out that what we have given teens are two "wildly divergent messages" (p. 157) in which the girls are to cultivate this hypersexualized image but abstain from actual sex. This reminds me of Rita, mentioned at the beginning of the first chapter, who began stripping with very little real-life sexual experience and yet perfected the simulated sex movements in her stage performance.

> They live in a candyland of sex . . . every magazine stand is a gumdrop castle of breasts, every reality show is a bootylicious Tootsie Roll tree. And these are hormonal teenagers: This culture speaks to them. But at school, the line given to the majority of them about sex is just say no. They are taught that sex is wrong until you have a wedding. . . . If you process this information through the average adolescent mental computer, you end up with a printout that reads something like this: Girls have to be hot. Girls who aren't hot probably need breast implants. Once a girl is hot, she should be as close to naked as possible all the time. Guys should like it. Don't have sex. (Levy 2005, pp. 157–158)

Of course, despite the latter part of this mixed-up message, adolescent girls are having sex. The pornified sexual look is a performance that garners attention, so advancing this performance into sexualized behavior will also continue to reward girls in the ways that they have been socialized to value themselves. The problem here is that "we are doing little to help them differentiate their sexual desires from their desire for attention" (Levy 2005, p. 162). Not a surprise when there is little sex education or guidance distinguishing images from reality or explaining sex, pressure to have sex, contraception, or sexual orientation. The porn image and behavior are consistent with "the message sent by the media to girls that they should always be sexually available, always have sex on their minds, be willing to be dominated and even sexually aggressed against" (Farley 2009, p. 146). Levy (2005) correspondingly documents her conversations with teens in which girls talk about engaging in sex because it helped them fit in rather than because they derived pleasure from it. The divorcing of sexual performance from sexual pleasure is yet another casualty of the contradictory messages and hypersexed images dogging the gender development of girls. This is sad, because (again, reminding me of Rita) from the very "beginning of their experiences as sexual beings they are conceiving of sex as a performance you give for attention, rather than as something thrilling and interesting you engage in because you *want* to" (Levy 2005, p. 163; emphasis in original).

Complex personhood (Gordon 1997) challenges static constructions of self and embraces possibilities for multiple and fluid identities that are rooted in ongoing negotiation. "Even those who live in the most dire circumstances possess a complex and oftentimes contradictory humanity and subjectivity that is never adequately glimpsed by viewing them as victims or, on the other hand, as superhuman agents" (Gordon 1997, p. 4). Complex personhood inhabits the "in between" spaces, where complicated human beings have daily, lived experiences that draw upon different meanings of our identities. Yet when I consider the experiences of adolescent girls in light of the increasingly pornified gender expectations, I am concerned that their power to lovingly tend to the developing complexity of their identities is dying on the vine, or at least being driven deeply underground. Instead, girls are growing up with what Tolman (2002) calls "confused bodies," in which strongly promoted sexual images and performance caricature reality and diminish skills in coping with intimacy and feeling. As discussed above, girls are already "embodied" through gender socialization. The emphasis on and preoccupation with the female body and its appearance are bound up in identity meanings. When these meanings are so woefully mismanaged by the social influences and institutions in a girl's life it is no wonder the (embodied) identity becomes confused. The confused body falls short of the possibilities opened up by the postmodern feminist notions of gender performance noted earlier in this chapter. Even though the pornified sexual image is an artificial construction, adolescent girls are provided fewer and fewer tools to see around it, beyond it, or through it. They are tightly bound by the fetters of the commodified adolescent experience to the constructed image, an image relentlessly reinforced everywhere they turn. Under these conditions, it is practically impossible to destabilize meanings of gender. Instead, adolescent girls *become* the pornified sexual performance in ways that have very real, damaging consequences on their bodies and their psyches. Later chapters will speak in greater depth about these effects.

3
The Processes of Sexualization

I knew it was wrong because I didn't like it. You know, when you don't know it's wrong you feel good about it, but that made me feel dirty. I mean, and I tried to not be pretty. I would wear my hair straight. I had big beautiful green eyes and I always wished I had black eyes. As a little girl. I mean, I'm OK with myself now. I always wondered if he was doing anything with my other sisters below me. One, I had kind of a suspicion. Me, I don't know why he did it to me. He always used to say I didn't belong to him. If mom and dad got in a fight, he would say, look at Sherie, she doesn't belong to me. —*Sherie, age 62*

Chapter 2 detailed the increasingly alarming aspects of gender socialization for girls, particularly in terms of the pornified sexualization that occurs in conjunction with the focus on female embodiment. I have argued that with the ratcheted-up levels of sexualization and the saturation of this image in the market, it is more and more difficult for girls to carve out different meanings of identity for themselves. Also important to add to this discussion is that girls are far from a monolithic entity with identical experiences. Instead, individual lives are affected by a range of personal, day-to-day aspects of existence as well as by larger structural realities of inequality and disenfranchisement (or privilege and advantage). At one end is the pornified sexualization that occurs as part of girls' gender socialization and identity development, as discussed in the previous chapter. The opposite end of the continuum represents the more directly traumatic and dangerous aspects that include sexual abuses and violence against women and girls. All of the remaining sexualization experiences fall between these ends. Though it is a relatively straightforward concept, many factors affect the scope and type of experiences an individual girl or woman has along the continuum of sexualization.

For instance, I noted above that it is important to locate the continuum of sexualization within larger structures of relative privilege or disadvantage. Even though individual experiences are usually felt on a deeply personal level, they are still situated within a variety of contexts. Heightened or lowered risks along the continuum may be correspondingly affected not just by individual factors but by structural conditions and intersections of marginalization related to race, class, sexual orientation, social exclusion, and the like. This chapter will round out the scope of experiences that can fall along the continuum of sexualization; first it will examine in greater depth issues of sexual violence and abuse. It will then integrate contextual factors that can exacerbate risks of this sort by engaging more findings derived from the two case study populations of exotic dancers and homeless women.

Sexual Abuse and Violence

Since the previous chapter focused on the ways that sexualization is impressed upon young girls as a part of gender socialization, a more comprehensive perspective of the continuum of sexualization is achieved by looking at the ways such constructions emerge in contexts of violence. Existing reports of childhood sexual abuse (CSA) are telling in this regard. Boys are victimized by CSA, but girls experience this type of abuse at higher rates (Chesney-Lind & Irwin 2008). The Bureau of Justice Statistics (Snyder 2000) determined that 86 percent of all victims of sexual assault are female—including 69 percent of victims under 6, 83 percent of victims under 12, and 82 percent of victims under 18. Other studies corroborate these numbers (Heger et al. 2002). A stark reality that further supports the higher rates of female sexual victimization is that girls—especially younger ones—are most often the victims of family members. For instance, only 3 percent of offenders in sexual assaults of children under the age of 6 were strangers (Snyder 2000). Estimates range from one-third and one-half of girls' sexual abuse being intrafamilial compared to one-tenth and one-fifth of boys' victimization (Finkelhor 1994). Bringing together these numbers shows us that even the youngest victims of CSA are girls and are predominately being abused by family.

Findings from the National Violence Against Women Survey (Tjaden & Thoennes 2000) indicate that 9 percent of surveyed women (N = 8,000) were raped before the age of 18. Of those raped, 21.6 percent of the women were under 12 and 32.4 percent were aged 12–17 when the rape occurred (Tjaden & Thoennes 2000). Child sexual abuse includes many behaviors in addition to rape, as it can involve contact (such as molestation and completed rape) or noncontact (such as exposure or masturbating in front of the child) victimization. When the two were combined, one study revealed that almost two-thirds (62 percent) of the women interviewed reported such experiences from childhood, with nearly half (45 percent) having endured contact CSA (Wyatt, Newcomb, & Rierderle 1993). Davis (1999) asserts that of girls 13 years old and younger, 60 percent experience involuntary sex in the form of incest, molestation, rape, or coercive sexuality.

Sexual abuse is underreported by both male and female children (Becker 1988), with some finding that no more than 2.4 cases in 1,000 are reported to authorities (Finkelhor 1994). There are a number of reasons why victims do not report or else delay their disclosure until adulthood (still others repress the memories or keep them secret). Primarily, this type of abuse is highly traumatic, and initial reactions to CSA include anxiety, depression, fear, anger, hostility, and inappropriate sexual behavior (Belknap 2007). Lack of disclosure can occur because child victims feel ashamed, they have no protection, they are afraid they made it up, they want to forget, or they may be blamed for their victimization (Bass & Thornton 1991). Perpetrators also use a range of coercive tactics to maintain the abuse and the silence of the victim, including bribes, threats (to harm or kill the child, a loved one, or cherished pet), or physical aggression (Barnett, Miller-Perrin, & Perrin 2005). It is important to remember, then, that the numbers we do know about the sexual victimization of girls only tell part of the story of the violence they experience.

Raising the Risks

Being a victim of child sexual abuse can increase the risk for more sexual victimization, and it most effectively does so because it raises the likelihood that girls will run away and seek early independence. Early independence is a permanent departure from the childhood home while at a young age. It is well documented that a substantial portion of homeless and runaway youth have experienced child abuse (see Janus et al. 1987; Silbert & Pines 1982; Tyler, Hoyt, & Whitbeck 2000; Whitbeck et al. 2001). Chesney-Lind (2001) notes that 70 percent of girls on the streets are running away from home to flee violence. Running away and early independence can create additional vulnerabilities to severe experiences along the continuum of sexualization, including exploitation and sexual victimization, as girls try to survive on their own and on the streets. Indeed, one study found that when girls were at a particularly young age the first time they left home, the likelihood increased that they engaged in strategies such as survival sex (having sex in exchange for protection, food, or some other essential) (Tyler et al. 2004). Survival sex is an example of what Schaffner (2006) calls "sexual solutions to nonsexual problems" (p. 81), something she finds to be a strategy often identified by scholars who examine the lives of vulnerable populations of young women. Pressing economic needs, early independence, lack of social supports, desperation, and danger, along with the cultural emphasis on pornified sexualization and expectations of (hetero)sexual availability, can all conspire to lead girls to turn to an older man or "boyfriend" to solve "many of their problems, such as procuring housing, transportation and food" (p. 81). Other studies find that sexually abused female runaways are more likely than either males or nonabused females to have engaged in deviant or delinquent activities such as substance abuse, petty theft, and prostitution (McCormack, Janus, & Burgess 1986). Sweet and Tewksbury (2000), in their study of twenty exotic dancers, discover that early independence was the most influential factor in choosing an exotic dancing career for the women they interviewed, and Monto and Hotaling (2001) found that a substantial number of prostitutes were minors when they began working.

Early sexual victimization and running away thus contribute to a pattern called "risk amplification" (Chen et al. 2004, p. 1), since the desperate need for survival options on the streets makes girls and women vulnerable to more victimization along the continuum of sexualization.

> Survival on the streets of any city is dangerous for a young woman. If she is too young to look for legal work or has too few skills to find work at a living wage, she has few choices other than to find a

"hustle" which will generate income for food and a place to sleep. Whether looking for shelter, panhandling, shoplifting, selling drugs or turning tricks, a young woman alone on the streets is often "fair game" for male violence. (Gilfus 2006, p. 10)

Trading sex or surviving through sex work is not just exploitive, it is extremely high risk; street prostitution in particular is dangerous. According to Raphael (2004), more than twenty research studies have documented an "almost unimaginable level of violence in street prostitution" (p. 100). A sample by the Center for Impact Research in Chicago of 113 female prostitutes on the Chicago streets found that 20 percent stated customers threatened them with a weapon, 22 percent had sex forced on them, 39 percent reported being slapped, and 33 percent punched (Raphael & Shapiro 2001). From these instances we can see how some experiences along the continuum of sexualization, such as sexual abuse, expose girls to even more danger. In general, child sexual abuse significantly increases the risk of subsequent sexual and physical victimization (Noll 2005). In the case of runaways, early independence due to childhood victimization reinforces the focus on the sexualized body as a means of survival. The female body becomes a commodity for the young girl on the streets.

> Most runaway girls have fled homes where abuse, including sexual abuse, was a prominent theme in their lives. Yet, ironically and tragically, their lives on the streets are almost always even more abusive in nature because, like all other aspects of life, the streets are gendered. Once on the streets, girls quickly discover both the dangers involved in street life and the narrow range of survival options available to them as girls. They also discover that they are in possession of a form of "sexual capital" they can access, while boys tend to engage . . . in a wider variety of survival strategies. (Chesney-Lind & Irwin 2008, p. 84)

In this way, the continuum of sexualization snowballs. For girls in desperate environs, the pornified, sexualized body is the only capital they have—but in tragic irony, this only reifies or compounds the same abject life circumstances they have been enduring.

In the lives of girls and women, the continuum of sexualization is contextually situated.

> "Context" is meant to signify a complex nexus of lived experiences, rather than one specific event or even a single enduring reality—

> gender inequality and oppression in a patriarchal society parlay into individual, institutional and structural marginalizations that contribute to women's lived experiences. For instance, individual women can endure sexual, physical and emotional degradation or victimization, be impacted by restrictive institutional access to resources and experience structural exclusions from economic power and social capital. (Wesely 2006, p. 304)

In other words, for each individual there are myriad factors that may or may not increase the risks for damaging events along the continuum. Other structural conditions beyond gender inequality contribute to the limitations on the healthy growth of girls and intersect with their experiences of sexualization. For example, Olfman (2009) notes that "the children who are most harmed by a sexualized culture are those who are already at risk because they are growing up with poverty or abuse" (p. 2). Indeed, poverty and socioeconomic class influence the ways in which girls' experiences fall along the continuum of sexualization. "Fewer alternatives and opportunities and thinner decisional avenues are available to poor girls than to their more affluent counterparts" (Schaffner 2006, p. 59). Vulnerability to predatory men, less access to legal protection, and limited resources are all ways in which poverty can affect outcomes for girls (Schaffner 2006). Racism and racial inequality also shape risks for girls in a highly sexualized society and can intersect with other oppressions. Scholars such as Raphael (2004), Schaffner (2006), and Miller (2008) discuss this in light of the disadvantaged populations of girls and young women they study. "The processes of oversexualization of this population of girls in trouble, facing racism and poverty in brutal ways, involve an imbalance between adolescent exploratory sexual activities and other, nonsexual preoccupations" (Schaffner 2006, p. 99). In her book *Getting Played: African American Girls, Urban Inequality, and Gendered Violence,* Miller (2008) examines "how structural inequalities that create extreme—and racialized—urban poverty facilitate both cultural adaptations and social contexts that heighten and shape the tremendous gender-based violence faced by urban African American girls. . . . Young women do their best to navigate these dangerous terrains, but they encounter vastly inadequate social and institutional supports" (p. 3). In the same vein, Schaffner (2006) notes that though African American girls aged 10 to 17 comprise about 7.5 percent of the national population and 44 percent of participants in her study, they were 100 percent of the girls in her sample that were arrested for sexual misconduct. Says Schaffner (2006),

> I attribute this disturbing fact, in part, to the dehumanizing processes of the hypererotic (and lucrative) popular-culture industry. That cultural dehumanization, coupled with disproportionately limited material avenues available to young black girls, produces a situation in which young women endure, clients enjoy, and arresting officers utilize their discretionary power. (p. 82)

Raphael (2004) finds that the "double bind of racism and poverty" (p. 140) plays a role in terms of the entry of economically deprived girls and women of color into prostitution as well as in the factors that complicate their exit. Gender and race inequality can be difficult to untangle from one another, and it has been noted that "sexism and racism combine with class exploitation to produce a three-edged mode of oppression for women of color" (Marable 2004, p. 163). This is certainly true in the urban neighborhoods where the girls in Miller's (2008) study reside—places characterized by "entrenched poverty, segregation, physical decay, and crime problems are dangerous places for young women" (p. 67), particularly in terms of gender-specific risks they face daily. In portions of these areas where groups of men and boys congregate, the girls navigate treacherous terrain. Miller (2008) found that the girls are victimized by men who predominantly view them through a sexualized lens and then are blamed (by others and themselves) for their victimization. "These widespread belief systems did not just affect youths' perceptions of gender and risk but contributed more broadly to a hierarchy on the streets in which females were situationally disadvantaged vis-à-vis males and therefore often viewed by males simply in terms of their sexual availability" (p. 39). In a culture that sexualizes girls and women of color in specific ways, dehumanizing constructions contribute to their degradation.

> Inestimable damage is done to society's humanity, and particularly to African American young women's sense of self, by the "controlling images" of a dominant media that present young women of color as oversexed or always ready for sex. Numbed by a barrage of hip-hop video images of "booty-shakin' mamas"—with little critical analyses or adult intervention—some young women who are relatively unprotected from misogyny experience popular culture uniquely. (Schaffner 2006, p. 84)

Hill-Collins (2008) talks about the race- and gender-specific violence and imagery experienced by and applied to African American women: "Treating African-American women as pornographic objects and portraying them as sexualized animals, as prostitutes, created the controlling image of the jezebel. Rape became the specific act of sexual violence forced on black women, with the myth of the Black prostitute its ideological justification" (p. 147). bell hooks (1999) has also extensively explored the constructions of black female sexuality that contribute to specifically framed pornified images and messages directed at women of color. With such limited portrayals, women of color have few "dominant alternative images, avenues for engagement, and material resources" (Schaffner 2006, p. 85). These struggles—the racism of sexual politics—contribute to the scope of experiences along the continuum of sexualization for girls.

To better unpack the continuum of sexualization within larger contexts, the rest of the chapter will draw upon the two different case study populations of exotic dancers and homeless women, both of which are groups with whom, as I mentioned previously, I have conducted in-depth qualitative interviews over the past decade (see the Appendix for research methods). For the purposes of this book, their lived experiences serve to illustrate ways in which the continuum of sexualization is contextually situated among particular marginalized populations and individuals within them. Both groups of women had young lives fraught with destructive lessons about what it meant to grow up female. Further, their childhoods were located within a context of social exclusion and a dearth of resources, social support, or stability. I do not suggest that all members of stigmatized or marginalized populations had dysfunctional or disastrous childhoods. I also do not claim that the two groups I discuss here have experiences that are a representative cross-section of all inequalities. Though the women I interviewed self-identified across a range of diverse ethnicities and sexualities, the overall intersectionality of what I was able to flesh out amid my findings concerning these specific topics is limited. Throughout the book I try to counteract these limitations by integrating results from other researchers about a range of populations of girls and women and the intersections of various inequalities. My purpose in this chapter is to engage the words of the women I interviewed to discuss what has happened in their lives, with attention to the overlap of the continuum of sexualization and limiting structural conditions characterized by few outside resources or support. It is important to discuss the powerfully degrading nature of the sexualization and abuse they endured while also living in environments that offered little guidance or intervention. Their experiences add to an overall understanding of the continuum.

Case Study One: Exotic Dancers

From qualitative, in-depth interviews with current and former exotic dancers, I gleaned extensive information about their lived experiences of sexualization that, for many of them, began early in their childhoods. Their narratives detail these experiences along the continuum of sexualization—experiences that were further rooted in contexts that structured the environments of inequality, disadvantage, and desperation in which the women grew up. These same contexts that situated their lessons in sexualization limited their viable options for livelihood as they moved into adult lives.

An array of behaviors contributed to the dancers' awareness of their sexual objectification as girls. Such experiences are not limited to those who become sex workers and are illustrative of how pornified sexualization becomes incorporated into meanings of power, identity, and the body. The women recalled learning at an early age that acting provocatively and emphasizing their sexuality could result in attention and reward. As Sheila described it, "I was always flirty, trying to get attention from men. In high school I was voted biggest flirt. . . . I always dressed sexy, and got all the attention." Responses from parents or other adults reinforced this behavior. Roxy said that in high school, "I would tease my mother, saying I'm going to pose in *Penthouse* [pornographic magazine]." Then, one day when Roxy got home from school, her mother was the one who informed her of a strip club that was hiring. Gina described a situation in which she used sexualized appearance and behavior to manipulate her male homeroom teacher while she was in high school:

> [The teacher] was the kind of guy that would stare at every girl's ass when she walked into the classroom. I mean, definitely a sexual harasser. Did it bother me? No. I used that to my advantage so I could walk into class 10 minutes late and not have to worry about it. I would shake my ass a little and smile at him. And he would never write me up. Now my sister had a problem with this

kind of attention, so she reported him for sexual harassment. But both of us got the same exact type of attention and, me, I took it as something to manipulate, whereas my sister took it as, ohmigod, he's looking at me in a creepy way, and I don't like it.

When I talked with Rita about the quote that began this book, I followed up by asking her, "So you use your sexuality, or your attractiveness, to get what you want?" She replied, "To open doors, oh yeah. And I use it. That's exactly how I get what I want. You gotta play the game." While playing this game gave the teenage Gina and Rita a sense of power derived from using their sexualized bodies, the game was, ultimately, a losing one. As they were soon to realize, the power they felt was fleeting, and privileges such as a late pass or a discount bear little impact on their abilities to change their life circumstances, so limited by the inequalities they faced. As Roxy said, "But when you make choices like [working at a strip club], you're looking at long-term damage. Because no education, nothing to fall back on. And of course, as fast as the money came, it went." Instead, then, these experiences along the continuum continued to spotlight the embodied, sexualized constructions of female identity at the exclusion of other, healthier possibilities.

Sure enough, the emphasis on these meanings took a more destructive turn along the continuum. The significance of the message that women must always be sexy or available for sex seemed magnified in the childhood homes of many of the interviewees. Marie remembered that her father "had a sexual addiction, and he ended up cheating on my mother and leaving her." Sheila recalls an early belief that after her mother's death when Sheila was 4 years old, her father remarried a particular woman just for the sex. One specific incident that stands out in her memory occurred when her stepmother greeted her father at the airport naked under a fur coat. "I remember always thinking in my head, I always got the impression that sex was what was important to a man. That's what men wanted. Even with my stepmom, we knew what [my father] was doing." Sheila also remembers her father's cold treatment of her and her interpretation that love and affection were only acquired via sex. She describes,

> All through my life before this, I would just have sex so I could get affection. And it was never really like, it was never good for me. I want attention, I want "acceptable," so that's what I did. When I

went to college, it was always clear to me that men just want sex. That's why they like you. You're always hoping for something more. But, you know, they would never have a relationship with you if you didn't have sex with them. So I always dressed sexy, and got all the attention.

Gina was devastated by the fact that her father cheated on her mother with a new woman who was "looser, sexier." She says,

> It was absolutely heartbreaking for me. I was definitely a daddy's little girl. It was heartbreaking when my mom and dad split up, and I think at that point I probably took it a lot like it was my fault or had something to do with me. I had kind of a shaky distrustful thing going on with my dad for awhile because my dad cheated on my mom and eventually married the woman he cheated on her with. . . . I can understand it now but at the time it was very much a betrayal, very devastating. I was left with the impression that my stepmother was much more adventurous, much more sexual. Whereas my mother, you don't talk about things like that.

Much like Sheila, Gina says, "So maybe, I think somewhere along the line it gave me the idea that that is how you win a man over, is through sexuality." She adds,

> I caught on very early that sexuality was definitely a way to go as far as getting attention. . . . I mean, I can remember being in 8th grade and thinking, I want to be a Playboy bunny when I grow up. I wanted to be a Dallas Cowboys cheerleader for the same reason. In 4th grade I was trying to wear tight Jordache jeans! 'Cause I knew if my butt looked good in them I would get more attention.

Along the continuum of sexualization, these examples became increasingly severe and damaging. Marie remembers that her father's pornographic magazines were on proud display all over the house, and she often examined the images inside. She said, "I could see how women were in *Playboy* magazines and how they were using their bodies. This said to me, this is how you get the maximum usage out of what you got." The porn magazines were the most "minor" of her father's transgressions: "He was the type of man that had to make comments about some girl's breasts, some girl's rear," and he critiqued his daughter similarly, especially her prepubescent chest. "Plus my father used to say to me all the time, all you need is Band-Aids for a bathing suit. Just put two Band-Aids here. Constantly said that to me." It is no surprise that Marie got breast implants as soon as she was able. This surgical procedure is external evidence of the lessons about being female that Marie learned as a child from the man in her life. Her father's overemphasis on women's pornified bodies through the magazines and his critical scrutiny of his little girl's breasts reinforced the fundamental contradiction with which Marie continued to struggle: the sexualized body is your only value as a woman, but it is never good enough.

Some aspects of sexualization the women experienced as girls and adolescents clearly seemed to teach them how to use their bodies to manipulate, get attention, and feel a form of power. But this power was short lived. More extreme forms of sexualization were explicitly violent and solidified opposing feelings of powerlessness. Nine—nearly half—of the women reported that they were molested or raped as children or teenagers (as with child sexual abuse in the general population, this number is probably underreported). Skye had a perspective that reinforced the frequency with which her fellow dancers had experienced sexual abuse: "We're all so much alike it's almost scary. In all the clubs I've worked at, about 97 percent of the girls I've worked with have a past similar [to mine]. Whether it be their own father, or a brother or an uncle, most of them have had some sexual abuse. Which is sad." Skye was raped three times by her father at the age of 12. Her father blamed her for the rape and forced her to attend church the morning after to confess her "sins," tragically illustrating the way girls are taught that they are responsible for their own victimization and degradation. Skye's mother also blamed her daughter, the victim: "After that incident, when he raped me, I shut up. . . . Then five years ago my mother confronts me with, well, you really should not have been wearing nightshirts."

Marie's father often exposed himself to her. "He would be sitting in front of you with his thing hanging out of his shorts. And when he abused me he would do it with my pants down. . . . And he would take me out of the shower and whip me with the belt, so I was naked when he hit me." Some, like Roxy, experienced molestation at a very young age. In her case, the memories did not surface in her consciousness until she was in her 20s.

That's kind of still . . . I remember things, but was that really memory? Things like inappropriate behavior, or other . . . did that really happen? Was I fantasizing? . . . The molestation, I think I was around four [years old]. I couldn't stand wearing dresses. I hated it. I remember my dad would grab me around the throat and just hold me there. And if I would struggle or cry he would just laugh, you know. So I quit crying.

Tragically, what I relay here are only a portion of the sexual victimizations the women recounted in their narratives. Such abuse was common among the women I interviewed. Sexual molestation and rape occurred at the hands of strangers, parents, and acquaintances of the women when they were children, teenagers, and young adults—typically multiple times. Valerie was sexually abused by her babysitter's sons when she was 5 years old and they were 12. She was also raped in her young adulthood one night when she was intoxicated:

This one time I went out and there was this guy that I knew from high school there. I knew he was attracted to me. I knew he paid my friend to leave. I had a few beers, a few more beers, and I was freaking sauced. I couldn't function. I tried to throw up in the bathroom and passed out. I was thinking, god, how many shots . . . and he took me home and had sex with me. . . . He took my tampon out of my body and had sex with me. . . . I remember thinking to myself, he is gross, and being really out of it, but remembering everything. And I know now, it was Rufies. The date-rape drug. There's no way I could have been that drunk.

Sheila was another woman who was sexually assaulted when she was not fully conscious; in this case, she was 15 when a man raped her while she was passed out.

I start drinking some beer, and this guy is like, have another beer. The guy says, come on, let's go get some beer, have another beer. And I'm like, OK. And then he's like, we'll go when you give me a kiss. I gave him a kiss, and next thing you know, I'm passed out, and he's raping me. I come to, sort of, and I'm like, take me home, take me home. My pants are ripped, there's blood. I walk in, I can't really say anything, 'cause I've been drinking and my stepmother doesn't really like me in the first place. So, hi, don't want to breathe on them, go take a shower.

She walked right past her family and on into her bedroom, never telling them because she knew they would not support her.

Indeed, the lack of intervention by adults and other authority figures in the women's lives was also commonplace. Often, the ones who were there to care for them as children were the ones who inflicted the abuse. Even in family situations that were not violent or severely neglectful, the parent or caregiver tried to raise them amid multiple obstacles, including unemployment or low-wage work, lack of transportation or childcare, economic hardship, health problems, or while enduring intimate partner violence. These factors create what Schaffner (2006) calls "empty families":

> Grave challenges often derail parents' abilities to guide and protect their daughters. Divorce, overwork, substance dependence, incarceration, mental illness, ill health, homelessness, and death were events that young women in my sample identified as reasons for the absences and ineffectuality of their mothers, fathers, grandparents, aunts, uncles, cousins, and siblings. These factors, not necessarily mutually exclusive, accounted for why girls wandered in empty families. Empty families are peopled, but the people are worn down, fighting their own battles, with little access to social, cultural, and economic capital, and simply unable to provide the protection and guidance their daughters need. . . . Families simultaneously and without relief faced severe, chronic, and multiple challenges—no income, no furniture, no food, involvement in the criminal and juvenile justice systems. (p. 87)

I find the "empty families" construct exceedingly helpful in informing my interpretation of the words of the women I interviewed, both among the exotic dancers and the homeless. Though certainly victimization played a major role in many of their childhoods, their families were also very much "empty" in the ways that Schaffner describes. If there was abuse, this emptiness contributed to the absence of recourse or support for the child victim. In her book on class, race, and family life, Lareau (2003) finds that parents' social location shapes children's life experiences. Rubin's (1976, 1994) work makes similar assertions about class inequalities and the ways in which our institutions maintain the continuity and stability of these divisions. This is especially pertinent to the women I interviewed, since without other supports or interventions, their childhood social locations and class status often sustained them in positions of disadvantage as they grew up.

The appeal of the sex work industry emerged out of these desperate environs. It is consistent with the above discussions of running away and early independence that some of the women found the money they received for their sexualized bodies to be their ticket to escape their violent homes. This is exactly what occurred with Skye:

> So I met this guy, through a friend, and he's much older than me, at the time he was 33, 34, and I was almost 14. He's working in this strip club, and I was hanging out with him a little bit, and I start meeting people he hangs out with. As soon as my parents are asleep, I'm out of there. One thing led to another, and next thing I'm on stage. I was seeing these girls with this kind of money, and I was living in a house I needed to get the hell out of. How do you get out of the house and survive unless you got money? Easy answer. . . . And that's pretty much how I started dancing. I did that enough to get me out of the house.

Skye began exotic dancing (illegally) at the age of 14. She also began prostituting and, between the ages of 14 and 18, having sex with male customers for money. When I asked her how many men this happened with, she replied, "That might scare me if I think about it. I'd say around ten." Skye capitalized on one of the few resources that she had control over—her sexualized body. By reducing her body to its exchange value in a patriarchal culture, she felt like she was able to control her immediate safety in the short term. So, amid the combination of extreme and damaging lessons along the continuum of sexualization, a desperation for escape or cash, and the absence of positive alternatives, the decision to become a sex worker evolved into a viable option. Though it provided her with some quick money, ultimately, however, it heightened her risks to further exploitation and victimization (this will be explored in greater depth in later chapters).

Structural conditions of economic marginalization thus combine with the gender inequalities that foster the continuum of sexualization. Tasha, for instance, began nude dancing at 18 when the electricity was turned off in the home she lived in with her mother. Ronai and Ellis (1989) note, "Financial crisis often served as the impetus for starting this occupation. Few have sufficient training or education to make as much money as other occupations" (p. 295). This was also the case for Rita, whose mother, as I first discussed in Chapter 1, began stealing from her bank account. It was at that point that Rita began dancing. Several of the women in this study who had worked as exotic dancers began doing so after being in foster care or to avoid homelessness. Irene recalls being placed into a state home at 15, along with her sister. By the time she was 18, she was out on the streets and was homeless for a period of time, living "on roofs and in stairways." She made the choice to begin dancing because of the money, saying, "Once I started doing it I did it everywhere I went." Irene danced for seventeen years to support herself but did not prostitute, because "it was so easy to make money dancing." As noted earlier, Paula also describes being neglected by her parents and ultimately "bounced from foster home to foster home—27 of them" during her youth. She states, "What keeps me dancing is the money. 'Cause I can make more in one night . . . in a good season, I can make $400–$600 a night." These lived experiences were located within structural contexts of disadvantage, poverty, and gender inequality that then shaped choices for these women. The effectiveness of this patriarchal legacy could potentially be mitigated by the availability and intervention of other social resources and influences (e.g., education, family, peer groups, service agencies), and I will explore this idea later on.

Case Study Two: Homeless Women

The second case study grew out of in-depth qualitative interviews that I conducted with homeless women residing in a shelter. This work originally was carried out as part of a larger project funded by the National Institute of Justice (NIJ) investigating violence and women's homelessness. My coauthors and I published *Hard Lives, Mean Streets: Violence in the Lives of Homeless Women* (Jasinski et al. 2010), which drew on the qualitative interviews as well as nearly 800 quantitative surveys with homeless women. Here I focus on information derived from the qualitative interviews (more about the quantitative surveys can be found in Appendix A of *Hard Lives, Mean Streets*). As with the experiences of the exotic dancers in the preceding section, I will begin here with a discussion of the backgrounds of the homeless women. They, too, reported sexual degradation and abuse during childhood. Such lessons were contextualized within conditions of structural disadvantage, including social exclusion and economic marginalization. Again, these contexts situate experiences along the continuum of sexualization, leading to higher risks of danger and exploitation as the women try to survive into adulthood. With lives marked by multiple deficits, including the dearth of social supports and practical resources characteristic of homelessness, their experiences along the continuum of sexualization were amplified.

Like the population of women who were exotic dancers, the women at the homeless shelter recalled receiving direct and explicitly sexualizing messages from parents and other adults around them during childhood. For example, several recalled hearing from mothers and fathers about how women were only good for one thing, and that one thing did not count for much. Eliza's father told her she should have been a boy, adding, "You're gonna grow up and be a whore and have a belly full of babies. And you're not gonna be any good." Feelings of worth were chipped away through these verbal assaults laced with hate of women. Both Ruby and Mo learned that men only wanted women for sex and that they should use their sexuality to their advantage. Mo remembers seeing her mother with many different male partners and reflects on a conversation when her mother told her, "Oh, if you ever want to get a guy's attention, wear this kind of stuff, act this way, do this." Likewise, according to Ruby,

> She didn't teach me to be—how can I put this—how to grow up. She never taught me how to depend on you and just do for you. She taught me to lay up with the men to get what I want. You know, I thought that's what I was supposed to do. I was supposed to go to bed with all these different men to get what I want. So I just figured that's what [women] were—I didn't know no better. That's what we were supposed to do. My mom always said we had a "money maker."

Through these lessons, the women learned that the sexually objectified body was a major part of their social worth or even livelihood, but that this body, paradoxically, was the source of their degradation and exploitation.

Along the continuum, these messages of sexualization compounded in severity, with twelve of the twenty women reporting sexual victimization as children (this number rises to sixteen when other forms of physical abuse are included). A range of studies corroborates that female homeless experience child sexual abuse at a higher rate than male homeless (McCormack, Janus, & Burgess 1986; Whitbeck & Hoyt 1999; Whitbeck and Simons 1990). Results from the Midwest Longitudinal Study of Homeless Adolescents (MJSHA) indicate significantly higher rates of sexual abuse among girls (32.1 percent) than among boys (10 percent) (Whitbeck & Hoyt 2002), and data from the Seattle Homeless Adolescent Research and Education Project (SHARE) reveal that females reported higher rates (44 percent) of child sexual abuse compared to males (18 percent) (Tyler & Cauce 2002). Although the narratives of the women I interviewed might sound sensationalized or extreme, they are not; far from the most "horrific" stories, these are, tragically, the relatively common lived experiences of the interviewees. Rena recounted a long history of sexual violence, beginning in third grade when she was raped by a school janitor. During her childhood, her mother attempted to kill her, her father molested and attempted to rape her, and she was gang-raped at age 14. Sara was physically abused by her father, mother, and siblings and molested repeatedly by her best friend's father when she was 8 years old. April was first molested by her stepuncle at age 2, a pattern that continued until she turned 13. Tamara was molested from the ages of 7 to 9 by a female family friend, was raped by her sister's husband when she was 14, and was beaten throughout her childhood by her father. Examples of a similar nature continue, but the experiences of Rena, Sara, April, and Tamara certainly illustrate the severe abuse that characterized the childhoods of the women.

Like the childhood experiences of the women described in the case study of exotic dancers, childhood victimizations of the women I interviewed at the homeless shelter were frequently ignored, even by close family members. This lack of intervention was often intensified by blame. Eliza tried to confide in her mother when her biological father began molesting her at age 7 or 8:

> I went into her room one day and I said, "Ma, I have to tell you something." She said, "What?" I said, "Daddy was touching me." She said, "What are you talking about? He wasn't touching you." I said, "Yes, he was, Ma. He was touching me." And she beat me. She beat me because [in her mind] I lied on my father.

Ruby's mother responded similarly when Ruby confided her father's molestation. "But she didn't ever believe me. She said I was a whore. She said I deserved it." Also absent were effective responses from institutions such as the criminal justice system. When April, molested from the ages of 2 to 13, finally came to the attention of the police, the information gathered was determined to be "insufficient evidence." She describes, "I was spending the night with my cousin when I was about 13 and I was mentioning it to her and she made me tell her mom and nothing ever came about it. They called the police, and [the perpetrator] got slapped on the wrist by the court system." Dee said she had told her mother about the sexual abuse she experienced at the hands of two teenage male cousins beginning when she was 5 or 6; the mother called the police on one of them, but that did not end the abuse. "We used to move around a lot," she said, "so that he wouldn't know where we were staying. But everywhere we moved, he always knew where we stayed and he always kept his promise" (to return and sexually abuse her). Not only did these minimal repercussions illustrate institutional lack of support, they also invalidated and minimized the abuse itself, effectively silencing the women.

Clearly, the women's narratives reflect childhood lived experiences along a continuum of sexualization that ranges from degradation to victimization. These experiences were rooted in larger contexts of structural disadvantage, especially in terms of economic hardship and social exclusion. For instance, many of the women recalled childhood homes that sometimes lacked even basic necessities of electricity or heat. Dee remembers having to use candles for light and being cold when the electricity in her childhood home was turned off, and Molly remembers the gas and electricity being off and the rent not paid. Eliza stated, "The house, nine times out of ten, we didn't have electricity. This is not painting this horrendous picture of this poor little black girl, it's just the way life was." These factors led to transience and displacement beginning at young ages. Further, as with the women who became exotic dancers, the childhood abuse experienced by the women discussed in this section also provided the impetus for early independence. Eliza, for instance, lived with her mother, father, and siblings until she was 7. Because of her parents' violence and drinking, at 7 she went to live with her uncle for a year. After returning to her parents at age 8, she was removed by the state and sent to a children's home. After a year or two, she was sent back home, where she was molested by her father and physically, verbally, and emotionally abused. She was beaten by her mother when she tried to confide her father's abuse. The parental neglect led her to wander the streets at night looking for food and a little bit of care. This began Eliza's trajectory toward "sexual solutions to nonsexual problems." The first older man she met at age 13 or 14, who fed her when she was hungry, became the father of her first two children. He was both a drug addict and abusive:

> He said, "What's your name?" He was real nice; he had a pocket full of money, wallet full of money. It was a summer night and I got in his car and I felt safe. And we rode over to where we ate. And he actually fed me and I was actually full. . . . He would feed me. I would be hungry. And I would still go home and act like this kid I was. But I'd get hungry. And sometimes there wasn't a pot of beans or some bread in the oven and I'd go find it. And he'd say, "You eat?" And I'd say, "no." And he'd say, "Let's go get something to eat." He fed me. . . . But again, it was a nightmare. It was a daydream, waking up from a nightmare, because I thought he was just so nice, and then after I gave up my virginity and the babies started coming, he wasn't so nice anymore.

Unfortunately, early independence typically exposed the women to even more violence and victimization. In *Hard Lives, Mean Streets*, we discussed findings from the quantitative surveys that indicated women who left their childhood home owing to violence were 30 percent more likely to experience adult physical violence. They were also more likely to experience multiple types of violence, compared to women who remained at home. Survival strategies of prostitution and exotic dancing were also more than twice as likely to occur among the women who left a violent childhood environment (Jasinski et al. 2010). Such high-risk survival options for homeless women are "intricately connected to women's subordinate position in society where victimization is coupled with economic marginality" (Gilfus 2006, p. 13). Despite these risks, it appears that leaving an abusive childhood home is typically viewed as more favorable than remaining.

In fact, some of the women found homelessness preferable to being in an abusive home. Quantitative findings from the original study reinforce the fact that childhood violence was significantly related to the women's experiences of early homelessness; women who experienced minor or severe childhood violence were on average 3 years younger when they first become homeless, and they were homeless more frequently and for longer periods of time (Jasinski et al. 2010). There is little doubt that running away and early independence contributed to the women's economic instability. Sara, who left home because of severe abuse and had a child at the age of 15, says, "But I guess being at the age of 14, 15 years old, you can't fend for yourself, you can't get a job, nothing." Mo recalled that she became homeless the first time to escape her abusive father:

> I just know I kinda left for a little while and [my father] didn't know where I was for about two or three years. I did that on purpose. I didn't contact no one in my family for a long time. . . . In my case, sometimes it was a choice because I didn't want to be found. I didn't want nobody to know me so it was easier to be homeless.

Though she frames it as a "choice," the fact is that when the two options are either being trapped in a violent home or being homeless—both dangerous and frightening situations—there is no alternative that provides for a positive, healthy, safe environment. Nothing that Mo "chooses" is then truly to her benefit; it is simply what she perceives to be the lesser of the evils. It helps to see these as "structured choices," because "circumstances have limited the agency of these girls at critical turning points in their lives" (Pettiway 1997, p. xxx). Indeed, within the overlapping and multiple contexts of deprivation, poverty, and social exclusion that root the continuum of sexualization in the childhood lives of the women, the move away from violence ought not to be constructed as an active move toward homelessness. Instead, it must be seen as survival.

Context and the Continuum

The case studies of exotic dancers and homeless women in this chapter provide two illustrations of how the continuum of sexualization can be contextualized within larger structural conditions and institutional arrangements, in this case putting them at higher risk for destructive experiences of sexualization. It is difficult to deny that both populations face numerous constraints related to economic marginalization and social exclusion that filter into their individual, day-to-day experiences and affect the vulnerability of each girl to everything from the pornified sexualized image to sexual abuses and violence. It is from within those disadvantaged contexts that events along the continuum are shaped and identity meanings are negotiated for these women. Of course, one limitation of using the experiences of multiply marginalized populations to address the continuum of sexualization concept is that by studying those already at risk, the argument can be made that their lives are not representative of the other populations of women, like those with "conventional" or privileged lifestyles. That is rather beside the point, since my goal in this chapter is to explore the situated nature of the continuum rather than to generalize about any or all groups of women. Even within the populations I discussed, there is no one, unifying experience. The women, though multiply disadvantaged, all had different lives. It is fair to say, however, that the severity of the deficits in their lives due to structural conditions and inequalities contributed to their vulnerabilities along the continuum of sexualization. The sheer amount of victimization and exploitation they endured as an already at-risk population is significant. At the same time, the experiences of both sets of interviewees demonstrate what occurs in the lives of many young women in our society to varying degrees. We must take their experiences as a lesson in the permanent damage done by the continuum of sexualization, especially when so many disadvantages coalesce. The next chapter will discuss the range of personal and social consequences of the continuum of sexualization on girls and women.

4

Personal and Social Consequences

Nobody gives a shit about what's in my head or what I said. It is all about the body. It is my tool, and I used that tool to pay my rent and get my drugs. I didn't feel connected greatly with it. And the things that started happening to me in my sex life: just another person who wants a part of this body. . . . I've never really had great sex at all. I guess I was the typical girl who thought sex and intimacy would bring her happiness. And it never has. Maybe that even started as early as my first sexual encounter. He may not keep me around after this, I may just be usable trash, but at least I made my impact. —*Julie, age 28*

A range of experiences along the continuum of sexualization are part of the everyday lives of girls and women. These experiences include the pornified sexualization absorbed via the process of gender socialization as well as increasingly dangerous degradations, exploitation, and abuse. Chapter 3 identified how the continuum of sexualization can be situated within a scope of structural and institutional contexts, which then shape each individual's lived experiences. In this chapter, the focus is on the many consequences of the continuum of sexualization on women and girls. It is important to note that the continuum is highly dynamic, with interplay between different experiences that fall along it. For example, the images and behaviors generated by the pornified sexualization aspect of gender socialization play a role in the epidemic of sexual violence against women and girls. In some ways, then, one experience along the continuum (sexual violence) might be seen as an effect of another experience (sexualization). At the same time, sexual violence against women along with the historical indifference and tacit tolerance for these sorts of crimes is also a testament to the societal desensitization to and mainstreamed nature of the pornified sexualization of girls. These realities, and others, emphasize the complex nature of the continuum. For the sake of clarity, however, this chapter will progress in a fairly linear fashion, streamlining a discussion of the consequences of the continuum of sexualization. As the sections progress, I will complicate notions of the continuum by foregrounding the interplay between its manifestations and effects.

Starting with Sexualization

As discussed in Chapter 2, as part and parcel of gender socialization, girls are reduced to certain embodied meanings, particularly in terms of sexualization. Ratcheted up in recent years, the images and behaviors conveyed and then internalized by girls have become increasingly pornographic. Further, these images are omnipresent, saturating entertainment, marketing, and consumption. On a most basic level, girls learn to "self-sexualize," which occurs "when girls think of themselves primarily or solely in sexual terms or when they equate their physical appearance with a narrow, often unattainable, standard of beauty" (West 2009, p. 90). The *Report of the APA Task Force on the Sexualization of Girls* calls this "self-objectification," which it defines as

> a key process whereby girls learn to think of and treat their own bodies as objects of others' desires. . . . In self-objectification, girls internalize an observer's perspective on their physical selves and learn to treat themselves as objects to be looked at and evaluated for their appearance. Numerous studies have documented the presence of self-objectification in women more than men. Several studies have also documented this phenomenon in adolescent and preadolescent girls. (APA 2007, p. 2)

Much like Foucault's panoptical self-surveillance described in Chapter 2, girls get the message that they must vigilantly monitor their appearance and shape their behavior in accordance with these pornified expectations. When there are few countervailing forces or little healthy information to challenge the one-dimensional but venerated pornified construct, the overemphasis on and preoccupation with the appearance of the female body has major adverse effects on girls and women.

Simply growing into adolescence seems to cause "girls who previously seemed resilient [to] become preoccupied with perfection" (ABA & NBA 2001, p. 9). As I noted in Chapter 2, these expectations are taking hold of girls at earlier and earlier ages (recall the discussion of tweens and prosti-tots). The American Psychological Association (APA 2007) reports a range of potential individual effects on girls due to their sexualization. Cognitive consequences include a decreased ability "to concentrate and focus one's attention, thus leading to impaired performance on mental activities such as mathematical computations or logical reasoning" (p. 3) and emotional problems such as shame, anxiety, or self-disgust. The APA *Report* finds that the three most common mental health problems associated with sexualization are eating disorders, low self-esteem, and depression. Attitudes and beliefs are affected as girls internalize their objectification, and such narrow ideals of female attractiveness affect boys as well, since it "may make it difficult for some men to find an 'acceptable' partner or to fully enjoy intimacy with a female partner" (p. 3). Among individual effects, the APA also reports that the sexual well-being of girls, such an essential part of healthy development, also plummets due to their sexualization.

This decline in overall sexual health is explored in the book *The Triple Bind* by developmental psychologist Stephen Hinshaw (2009), who discusses the contradictory pressures that confront today's adolescent girls. An aspect of his research recounts the damage to identity that results when teenage girls struggle to grow into healthy, whole sexual beings while living in a society in which the focus is on pornified sexual performance. Hinshaw (2009) points out that these expectations for girls do not allow them to develop and explore their own sexual desire. "The problem is that this new sexualization actually keeps girls from connecting to their sexuality—or, for that matter, to any true identity" (p. 110). Healthy sexual development is vital to a complete sense of self. Orenstein (1994) calls this "sexual entitlement" and states that it signifies "a sense of autonomy over one's body and desires" (p. 56) and is essential to a healthy and whole adult identity. If a girl does not have the opportunity to develop in this way, her oversexualization paradoxically results in *delayed* sexualization.

Unable to developmentally flesh out differences between sexuality and sex object, girls learn to *act* the part without feeling it. "She won't learn how to tap into her sexuality as a positive, empowering force . . . she may know how to look like she's doing those things. She may even be very good at faking them. But the connection between going through the motions and feeling the emotion will be lost" (Hinshaw 2009, pp. 112–113). This connection is a key aspect to women's psychological health.

The disjuncture between healthy sexuality ("feeling the emotion") and sexual performance ("going through the motions") discussed above is in reference to an epidemic problem affecting teenage girls. In Levy's (2005) conversations with this population, she finds that although it has always been typical for adolescents to try on and play with a growing awareness of a sexual self, there is "now a rigidly specific message girls are required to convey before they even grasp its meaning" (p. 152). The infusion of the pornified sexualization expectation into the everyday lives of girls is an eerie echo of what the women described as their work in the strip club:

And it's like role playing. I was a chameleon. So there's no real identity there. I don't think I ever really built up my self-esteem or my security level. You can't live a lie. You can pretend for awhile. That's why you have the stage. And once it's gone, it's gone. You can't pretend forever. . . . I'm 29 and still picking up scraps from 23, 24. (Roxy)

The fracture between sexualized performance and sexuality is complicated, because as the pornified image becomes elevated, there is no parallel increase in information about or attention to the development of girls' actual sexual desire. In her book *Dilemmas of Desire*, Tolman (2002) points out that little research has been done about the development of sexual desire in adolescent girls. Tolman explains that sexual desire is socially constructed as uncontrolled, uncivilized, and masculine—at odds with conventional expectations of femininity. Indeed, women's sexual desires have been cloaked in heterosexual romantic expectation, the only socially acceptable outlet for women's energies in adult relationships. These social conceptions underpin the "double standard" in our treatment of sexuality among boys and girls—that male sexual activity is expected or rewarded and girls' is shamed and ostracized. Further, because intense sexual desire is seen as "a natural and normal part of male adolescence and male sexuality . . . it is adolescent girls whom we hold responsible, because we do not believe boys can or will be" (Tolman 2002, p. 15). The reins of control and surveillance over girls thus tighten. As with other aspects of gender socialization, the control of female sexuality is a key component of the oppression of women (Rich 1976; Tolman 2002). The denial of female sexual desire and surveillance of behavior, along with objectification and pornified sexualization, serve to reinforce the framing of girls in rigid, limited categorizations that curtail individual agency and reinforce stereotypic expectations of women.

When acknowledged at all, the sexuality of teenage girls is discursively invoked in terms of physical risks (e.g., sexual violence, pregnancy, or disease), which further reinforce the social imperative for control and surveillance of the female body. It is true that adolescent girls do bear the brunt of physical consequences for unprotected sex, both in terms of pregnancy and disease. Yet, as Tolman (2002) points out, if this were our only concern, we would be pouring funds into effective, accessible forms of birth control and comprehensive sex education. Instead, sexualization not only eclipses but appears to replace all manner of healthy sexual knowledge and exploration for girls, as with Sheila:

No one told me about getting my period. I'm not even prepared. My step mom would go meet my father at the airport, and she would just have on a fur coat! Just to the airport, a fur coat with nothing under it.

Sheila makes side-by-side comments about her menstrual cycle and her stepmother that seem to form a non sequitur, but there is an underlying significance that connects them. Sheila's lack of information about her body and its functions as she physically matured into an adult woman is juxtaposed with the choreographed sexual performance she witnessed. These are the lessons she learned (or did not learn) about sexual development.

So how does a girl develop a sexual identity when she must leave "real" sexuality out? She doesn't. In her research with adolescent girls, Tolman (2002) finds that, whether or not they had sex, some girls did not recognize sexual desire or feeling in themselves, developing what Tolman calls "silent bodies." Other girls experienced "confused bodies." Confused bodies are those upon which the inherent contradictions between sexualization and sexuality are writ. Not sure if what they feel is sexual desire, girls with confused bodies struggle with the social constructions of femininity and sexualization in the context of their own lived experiences. These configurations tell us that girls have become disconnected from their own sexuality. The girls in Tolman's study who are able to access their feelings of sexual desire must still negotiate on an individual level how to situate these feelings within acceptable femininity. They see it as *"their own sexual feelings* that constitute both the problem and the answer. These girls all evidence awareness, at some level, that if they bring their desire forthrightly into their relationships, they will be in conflict with others in their lives, and with themselves" (p. 115; emphasis in original). Though experienced as deeply personal, such conflicts are based on the larger gender order, or as Tolman states, "the rule book of gendered sexuality, by the carrot of romance and the stick of a maligned reputation" (p. 115).

Sexual feelings are burgeoning in teenage years as part of biological maturity, but the flat-out dismissal of sexuality does little to help girls navigate this unfamiliar terrain. All the while, the message to appear sexy is bombarding them. These confounding lessons do not stop girls from having sex. Instead, the situation raises the likelihood that girls do not know how to handle sexual pressure, how to convey a desire to delay intercourse, or how to receive affection or have a relationship without sex. "Banishing sexual feelings dissuades girls from considering the numerous ways other than intercourse in which they might explore their desire, ways that might be more appropriate, more fun, and certainly less risky to their health" (Orenstein 1994, p. 57). It also raises the likelihood that they do not feel like agents in making decisions about their own sexual behavior, which leads to disengagement and passivity, at best, when confronted with sexual situations. Indeed, one study finds that a negative effect of sexualization is diminished sexual health for girls in the form of decreased condom use and decreased sexual assertiveness (Impett, Schooler, & Tolman 2006). These factors reflect the likelihood that, because of the absence of certain information and skills, girls have unsafe and risky sex.

Such concerns for girls in our society play out startlingly in the numbers. Despite (or more likely, because of) the meager education teens do receive, which more often than not emphasizes abstinence, preserving purity, and waiting for marriage, they are still having sex. "Eighty percent of Americans become sexually active while they're still in their teens" (Levy 2005, p. 160), and if the trajectory continues, this number will continue to increase. And becoming sexually active in adolescence does not necessarily refer to the "late" teens. The Centers for Disease Control (CDC) found in 2005 that one-third of ninth graders (age fourteen) had already had sex (Olfman 2009). The CDC also reports that in 2009, 46 percent of high school students had had sexual intercourse, and 14 percent of high school students had had four or more sex partners thus far in their life (CDC 2010). Some point out that teens' emotional maturity has not evolved at a comparable rate. "If children were really getting older younger—if they were actually going through all of the processes of physical, cognitive, social and emotional maturation more rapidly—then perhaps there would be little cost to them. But that doesn't seem to be the case" (Linn 2009, p. 47). Instead, teen girls, in particular, incur incredible costs.

For example, the Centers for Disease Control issued a press release in November 2009 entitled "CDC Report Finds Adolescent Girls Continue to Bear a Major Burden of Common Sexually Transmitted Diseases." In this report, the CDC finds that adolescent girls ages 15–19 years had the largest reported number of chlamydia and gonorrhea cases when compared to any other age group:

> While adolescent males have a similar prevalence of STDs, biological differences place females at greater risk for STDs than males. Additionally, the health consequences are more severe among females than males for chlamydia and gonorrhea—the two most commonly reported infectious diseases in the United States. These diseases may have no symptoms and often go undetected. CDC estimates that half of new gonorrhea cases and more than half of new chlamydia cases remain undiagnosed and unreported. Left untreated, it is estimated that 10–20 percent of chlamydia or gonorrhea infections in women can result in pelvic inflammatory disease, which can lead to long-term complications, such as chronic pelvic pain, ectopic pregnancy (a potentially life-threatening form of pregnancy where implantation of the fertilized egg occurs outside the uterus) and infertility. Untreated STDs are estimated to cause at least 24,000 women to become infertile each year in the United States. (CDC 2009)

It is perhaps not surprising, then, that the CDC also found that 34 percent of currently sexually active high school students did not use a condom during their most recent sexual intercourse (CDC 2009). Levy (2005) notes that while across the developed world sexual activity among adolescents is relatively stable, the United States has one of the highest rates of teen pregnancy. With Japan and most western European countries holding at teen pregnancy rates of about 40 per 1,000 and Holland at 12 per 1,000, the United States has more than 80 per 1,000. A country rich with resources, the United States has pregnancy rates on par with much more disadvantaged countries such as Bulgaria and Romania. These alarming realities certainly illustrate some repercussions of the climate in which girls are growing up.

Intracontinuum: Sexual Violence as an Effect of Pornified Sexualization

> I was not sexually abused. Yet I was sexually abused. We were all sexually abused. The images and attitudes, the reality we breathe in like air, it reaches us all. It shapes and distorts us, prunes some of our most tender, trusting, lovely and loving branches. We learn that this is who a woman is. This is what men think of women. This is what we are taught to think about ourselves. (Bass & Thornton 1991, p. 53)

Echoing the sentiment above, Dines (2010) points out that current culture is so sexualizing that all women are victimized by this faceless perpetrator.

> By inundating girls and women with the message that their most worthy attribute is their sexual hotness and crowding out other messages, pop culture is grooming them just like an individual perpetrator would. It is slowly chipping away at their self-esteem, stripping them of a sense of themselves as whole human beings, and providing them with an identity that emphasizes sex and de-emphasizes every other human attribute. (Dines 2010, p. 118)

In support of this argument, Dines points out that many of the damaging effects of sexualization result in the same symptoms as those manifested by sexual assault survivors, including risky sexual behaviors, eating disorders, depression, low self-esteem, and reduced academic performance. As such, "we appear to be turning out a generation of girls who have been 'assaulted' by the very culture they live in" (2010, p. 118):

> And there is no avoiding the culture. The very act of socialization involves internalizing the cultural norms and attitudes. If the culture is now one big collective perpetrator, then we can assume that an ever-increasing number of girls and women are going to develop emotional, cognitive and sexual problems as they are socialized into seeing themselves as mere sex objects and not much else. (Dines 2010, p. 118)

Sexualization, then, is its own victimization of girls and women. As part of an entrenched social order that preserves dominant power relations (that we all learn via gender socialization), sexualization generates and reflects sweeping social attitudes towards women and girls. The APA report calls for more research into the associations between sexualization and the sexual exploitation of girls, since such study is "virtually nonexistent" (APA 2007, p. 5). In an effort to investigate these associations, in the current section I will explore the idea that the social ideologies and attitudes that support the pornified sexualization of girls and women also contribute to direct, physical sexual violence against them. Since the impetus (pornified sexualization) and the result (sexual violence) both fall within the continuum of sexualization, this could be framed as an "intracontinuum" effect.

Rape, molestation, and other forms of sexual violence are powerful social weapons that preserve the status quo. They are instruments of power, "inflict[ing] damage through sexual means: rapists speak of the experience as an aggressive act of dominance, associated with power, rather than a particularly sexual act" (Reid-Cunningham 2008, p. 280). Eigenberg (2001) notes that "patriarchal social structures effectively use violence against women as an important means of social control" (p. 1); that is, violence or the threat of violence to keep women "in their place." Research about women's victimization finds that it "occurs within a wider context composed of responses from social agencies and general beliefs and attitudes about the relationships between men and women, husbands and wives, and about the use of violence to achieve various aims" (Dobash & Dobash 1998, p. 9). In essence, the standard ideologies that reduce girls and women to embodied, objectified meanings can also contribute to severe, violent outcomes in the form of molestation, rape, and other sexualized violence against them.

One aspect of the pornified sexualization of girls and women that can contribute to sexual violence is the confused interpretation that a sexy appearance or performance means that sex is first and foremost on the individual's mind, that sexual interaction is available if not wanted and desired, or that it is being *asked for* or invited. As discussed earlier, Valerie was raped while under the influence of a date-rape drug by a man she had known in high school. She attributes the sexual attack to how perceptions of her sexual availability change when people learn she was a dancer. Her interpretation is that her sexual performance is conflated with sexual willingness or even simply with open access to her sexual body.

> Once they find out you're a dancer, their motives change even more. Every guy wants to sleep with you if he's interested in you; you don't have to be a dancer for that. But it was like the dancer element added, like, they had a right: "That's what you do." It was an excuse for them to be extra aggressive. They actually legitimized it in the back of their mind. Women get no respect anyways, but when you're a tittie dancer, it makes it OK: "You're a slut anyways."

Using the interpretation that sexualized appearance, behavior, or performance is perceived as actual sexual accessibility, Valerie comes up with an explanation that connects one end of the continuum—sexualization—to another—sexual violence and violation.

> To dress the skankiest, I know that sounds terrible, but that would be the one way we all compete. Since seventh grade, the skankier, the smaller, the more cleavage, the better. . . . I wasn't particularly sexual then [in seventh grade] but I wanted guys to want me, to want to hook up with me, I guess . . . even though I didn't want to hook up with them. I always wanted all the guys to think I was the hottest one. (Levy 2005, p. 152)

The quote above is from Anne, one of the white-upper-class private high school teenage girls interviewed by Levy. I do not mean to suggest that Anne and Valerie are the same or that the teenage girls in Levy's book are no different from the exotic dancers in mine. What is the same—where these circles overlap—is in the significance of the performance. For girls like Anne, pornified sexualization has taken hold within the successful performance of looking "skanky." As Levy (2005) points out, wanting to be pretty and popular is one thing. Wanting to be the "skankiest"—"which means the smuttiest, the loosest, the most wanton" (p. 154)—is a new development among teenage girls, a further testament to the infiltration of pornified sexualization in our culture. And, I would argue, far more frightening in terms of legitimating, in the minds of perpetrators, sexual access to girls and women.

Valerie challenged me to perform an experiment:

> You should do a little test. Meet a guy in a club, and just tell him, "Oh, you want nothing to do with me!" "Why not?" "Well, 'cause I'm a topless dancer." Just watch his face change! Just say, "Oh, I'm Jennifer, bla bla bla, what do you do? Well, I don't want to tell you what I do, you'll think different of me." "No, I swear I won't!" . . . they say stuff like that. And say, "I'm a topless dancer." Just watch his face light up, and change. Just watch him change into a totally different person. Just go to a club and do that a couple times. Find someone you know is attracted to you, and watch his eyes light up. What that guy that the [rape] happened with, I knew him for years, in high school. But once he knew I was a dancer, he changed. He changed. There was this element in him, he had to have me. He felt like he had the right.

An exotic dancer engages in a sexualized performance that highlights her value as an object for the visual (and sometimes physical or emotional) consumption of customers. There is an element of possession and ownership over the object consumed, an element that Valerie addresses when she says, "He felt like he had the right"—the right to her body, sexually. Still, the fact that Valerie is or is not a dancer seems not to be the real issue. What Valerie's "test" suggests is that the social interpretations of the pornified, sexualized performance can reduce all girls and women to mere objects of sexual consumption and, ultimately, possible victims. In general, it speaks to the potential victimization that can result when perpetrators choose to interpret pornified sexualization as a green light for sexual access.

Also often implicit in pornified sexualization is the blurring between girl and adult woman, a factor that contributes specifically to child sexual abuse (CSA):

> Society has been blamed for encouraging CSA through advertisements, media, and pornography, which frequently blur distinctions between adult women and girl children—women are photographed to look childish, and girls are photographed to look sensuous. . . . Such forms of entertainment perpetuate the myth that children are willing participants and are not being assaulted, abused, exploited,

and raped when they have sex with adults. In reality, children are not in a position to make decisions about sex with adults. (Belknap 2007, pp. 283–284)

The sexualization of children is not the only factor in the perpetration of CSA. Nonetheless, the cultural milieu in which CSA occurs is one that condones the pornified sexualization of children, promotes sexiness by blurring lines between young girl and adult woman, and bulldozes this image into every possible venue. Dines (2010) described a conversation she had with a man currently in prison for raping his ten-year-old stepdaughter, who said it was "easy" to get his stepdaughter to "consent" because the "culture did a lot of the grooming for me." This perpetrator explained that the sexualized images to which his stepdaughter had been exposed from such an early age "as well as the sexualized conversations that such images generated in her peer group, had developed a precocious sexual curiosity that 'made grooming her easy'" (p. 118). As another case in point, girls are experiencing a variety of types of sexual violence at younger and younger ages. Hinshaw (2009) finds that there are increasing numbers of 10- to 12-year-old girls being sexually harassed, receiving unwanted sexual attention or pressure, and being raped. He notes that this problem is exacerbated by the portrayal of girls as sexual objects, which "tends not only to make girls objectify themselves but also to induce boys to view girls primarily as sexual objects intended for their gratification" (p. 119). The more desensitized and inured we become to these constructions of young girls, the more such heinous crimes are trivialized or ignored even as they escalate.

A society so inundated with sexual imagery, so complacent about and even complicit in the framing of girls as pornified sex objects, is one that automatically puts girls at risk for greater harm. How? First, I have noted that while the expectations for their pornified sexualization are amped up, girls are more disconnected from their sexual desire than ever. They may self-objectify and perform the sexy image, but sexual feelings remain underdeveloped and unexplored. This missing aspect of their identities is crippling, because silent and confused bodies are not active participants in sexual interactions. Saturated in oversexed imagery and expectation and while looking the part, girls may find themselves staring into a void when faced with decisionmaking about their bodies. As Tolman (2002) asks, "What 'choice' do girls have when their own sexual feelings are not supposed to exist?" (p. 203). Within sexual situations, then, girls become silenced. Ironically, in a culture that fixates on "risks" for sexually active girls, we have created a new category of vulnerability to sexual victimization.

> In other words, not feeling sexual desire may put girls in danger and "at risk." When a girl does not know what her own feelings are, when she disconnects the apprehending psychic part of herself from what is happening in her own body, she then becomes especially vulnerable to the power of others' feelings as well as to what others say she does and does not want or feel. (Tolman 2002, p. 21)

Without a sense of autonomy over their sexual health and desires, girls cannot be agents in their sexuality or truly assert what they want and—perhaps more important—what they do not want for themselves sexually.

Second, a path to violence against women typically begins with the successful reduction of human to object. When a person is able to be fragmented and reduced to her parts, she becomes dehumanized. It is the very process of sexualization—particularly in the form of sexual objectification, then—that removes women's humanity. Social learning theory (Bandura 1973, 1977; Bandura, Underwood, & Fromson 1975) supports the argument that dehumanization contributes to the justification of violence. In fact, "social learning theorists have argued for some time that dehumanizing others allows people to generate self-disinhibiting justification for cruel actions, whereas humanizing victims can have the opposite effect, that is, to strengthen such inhibitions" (Sommers & Check 1987, p. 190). In more recent work, Bandura (2002) discusses the issue of selective moral disengagement in the exercise of moral agency, finding that people are able to morally disengage from behaving inhumanely when there is an attribution of blame or dehumanization of those who are victimized. "Moral exclusion" (Opotow 2001) refers to the decision to frame violence directed at particular groups or people as appropriate, thus overriding other, more humane moral choices. Moral exclusion is supported by a range of social conventions and perceptual predispositions, among them three types of denial, one of which is the denial that excludes others.

> In moral exclusion, *denial that excludes others* is evident in such symptoms as dehumanization (denying others entitlements as well

as denying them their humanity and dignity), condescension and derogation . . . and biased evaluation of groups. (Opotow 2001, p. 156; emphasis in original)

Indeed, it is much easier to justify violation or exploitation of someone who is seen without identity or persona, without intrinsic human value. Arguments about dehumanization have long been attributed to the portrayal of women in pornography (Brownmiller 1975). Dines (2010) notes that "it is especially important for the pornographers to shred the humanity of the women in these images" (p. 63) because to be successful, porn must separate "porn women" from other women:

> The process of dehumanizing a group as a way to legitimize and justify cruelty against its individual members is not something that porn producers invented. It has been a tried and trusted method adopted by many oppressors. . . . Once the humanness of these individuals is collectively rendered invisible by their membership in a socially denigrated group, then it is that much easier to commit acts of violence against them. (Dines 2010, p. 65)

I have already explicated the ways that pornography has infiltrated the mainstream, so it is no surprise that the dehumanization of girls and women too has bled into everyday life. In her most recent film about the effects of advertising on women, *Killing Us Softly 4*, Jean Kilbourne (2010) compellingly demonstrates how women's bodies are turned into "things" in order to sell products. She argues that the dismembering, hacking apart, and fragmenting of women's bodies in ads is the first step toward dehumanization and creates a climate in which violence against women becomes normalized. Dehumanization occurs in racism, homophobia, and terrorism and has been a key strategy in mass atrocities, including not only the general massacre of entire populations but also the sexual violence and rape during World Wars I and II, the 25,000–50,000 estimated women systematically raped during the Balkan Wars of the 1990s, the 250,000–500,000 women raped in the summer of 1994 in Rwanda, and the mass rapes reported in Darfur and Democratic Republic of Congo in the last decade (Chang 1997; Heise 1998). In such contexts, "rapists often use dehumanizing epithets featuring racialized or gendered slurs directed at the raped woman and her community" (Reid-Cunningham 2008, p. 287) to justify the attacks. Sexual violence against women is a genocidal technique in the contexts of war and terror, but any rape is always a crime against humanity—even when the humanity of the victim is erased in the mind of the perpetrator.

A brief examination of certain sexual victimization rates drives home these points. Chapter 3 detailed the high amount of child sexual abuse going on behind closed doors. As noted in the current chapter, girls and adolescents are increasingly experiencing additional sexual victimizations, such as sexual harassment, at younger ages. One study of high school students who worked part-time found that about two-thirds of the girls reported sexual harassment at their jobs (Fineran 2002). A US government study found that 54 percent of identified raped women in the period examined were under eighteen years old (Rennison & Welchans 2000). Indeed, girls and women ages sixteen to twenty-four are the most frequent victims of rape (Belknap 2007). Date rape is especially prevalent as girls first strike out on their own, as when they begin to attend college; rape is particularly prevalent on college campuses. Keeping in mind the estimate that only 12 percent of rape victims report the crime (Foubert & McEwen, 1998), Belknap (2007) finds that roughly three-fourths of college women have experienced sexual victimization, including sexual harassment, and around one in four has experienced completed or attempted rape since the age of 14.

Consequences of Sexual Violence

Thus far, this chapter has discussed the effects of pornified sexualization of girls and women. As explicated above, sexualization both reflects and perpetuates social attitudes and ideologies that can also contribute to sexual violence. In addition, sexual violence has its own effects on girls and women. This section will first address these effects in a straightforward fashion as documented in existing research. It will then continue by challenging linear explanations of these effects and foregrounding the ways in which individual negotiation and social context play a role.

On an individual level, there are sets of short- and long-term effects that may be experienced by those who endured sexual victimization. A list of CSA effects can be found in almost any family violence or child maltreatment text. One excellent example is *Family Violence Across the Lifespan* by Barnett, Miller-Perrin, and Perrin

(2005). In their chapter on child sexual abuse, these authors detail behavioral, emotional, cognitive, and physical effects associated with sexual abuse in preschool, school-age, and adolescent children. Some common behavioral outcomes into adolescence include sexualized behavior and sexual preoccupation, seductive behavior, or promiscuity. Some common emotional effects include anxiety, nightmares, and depression. As victims of CSA age, they tend to have increasing difficulty with learning and concentration. The Barnett, Miller-Perrin, and Perrin text (2005) also enumerates long-term effects associated with CSA, with some of the most common being depression, anxiety, posttraumatic stress disorder (PTSD), sexual adjustment disorders, and behavior dysfunctions such as eating disorders, substance abuse, self-mutilation, and even suicide. Barnett, Miller-Perrin, and Perrin (2005) note that there are factors that may mitigate the severity of effects of CSA, though these again are typically identified only at the individual level. Potential mediators related to the nature of the abuse—its duration and frequency, the child's age at the onset, and the perpetrator's relationship to the child—play a role. Cognitive appraisals of the abuse and attributional styles (i.e., blame is attributed to self or attributed to the perpetrator) are psychological mediators, and specific postabuse events are also related to the effects of CSA, including the responses toward the victim by parents, other relatives, and teachers along with the availability of social supports.

Clearly, being sexually abused early in life makes girls and young women more vulnerable to a host of negative consequences on the individual level. It has already been established that there are differences in the rates of sexual abuse for girls and boys, with girls experiencing this type of violence at much higher rates. The effects of sexual violence are also gendered. For instance, boys and girls tend to respond to and cope with stress differently, with girls internalizing reactions by being depressed or withdrawn and boys by externalizing stress and acting aggressive. This is also clear in rates of substance abuse and relationships to sexual victimization. "Childhood maltreatment, including sexual and physical abuse, has a considerable impact on substance abuse among girls and young women" (CASA 2003, p. 50), since substance use is one coping strategy engaged in to avoid these painful childhood memories and reduce feelings of isolation (CASA 2003). When the life experiences of those in drug treatment programs are considered, more than twice as many girls as boys report physical or sexual abuse in the year prior to treatment (36 percent versus 16 percent), and "nearly twice as many girls in drug treatment who had a history of sexual abuse began using alcohol before the age of 11 compared to those who had no history of abuse" (CASA 2003, p. 51). According to CASA, sexual abuse also poses the greatest risk to the development of adult women's alcoholism, and more than two-thirds (70 percent) of alcoholic women seeking treatment have experienced some form of CSA compared to one-third (35 percent) of women in the general population. Women who were sexually abused as children are more than three times as likely to have symptoms of alcohol dependence and more than 2.5 times as likely to abuse drugs than those who had not been sexually abused (CASA 2003). These findings illustrate the gendered nature of one coping mechanism in response to CSA.

Though identity development happens throughout life, it is during early years that the foundation is laid (Josselson 1987, 1996). Trauma research (see Crowley 2000; Herman 1997) has established that when sexual violence happens to girls at a young age, they are violated at the same time that their (gender) identities are being shaped and their sense of self is coming to the fore. As a result, CSA can derail the healthy development of identity. The basic "psychological structures of the self and basic assumptions about oneself and the world are significantly affected by childhood experiences of incest" (Phillips & Daniluk 2004, p. 177). Child sexual abuse also challenges the assertion of appropriate personal and body boundaries. This can heighten the vulnerability of young adolescent girls to exploitation by predatory men. "Abuse can reduce a girl's capacity to recognize and protect her physical boundaries, especially when combined with the power differential inherent in sexual relationships between teenage girls and adult males (United Way of the Bay Area and the San Francisco Juvenile Probation Department 2003, p. 9). Herman (1997) identified the developmental processes of adaptation to sexual abuse that shape women's adult behavior: "Many survivors have such profound deficiencies in self-protection that they can barely imagine themselves in a position of agency or choice" (p. 112). Because clear boundaries have been repeatedly blurred by sexual abuse, survivors continue to grapple with where and how to assert these limitations—both psychologically and physically—as they grow up.

A plethora of research suggests that CSA victimization itself puts one at greater risk of adult sexual assault (Arata 1999; Messman-

Moore, Long, & Siegfried 2000; Neumann et al. 1996). Filipas and Ullman (2006), for instance, document the research finding that CSA survivors are at least twice as likely to be revictimized as women with no reported CSA. Noll (2005) corroborates that child sexual abuse significantly increases the risk of subsequent sexual and physical victimization:

> Thus, emerging evidence appears to suggest a persistent cycle of violence perpetrated against women that begins in childhood in the form of sexual abuse or exploitation, reemerges later in adolescence and early adulthood in the form of physical assault/domestic violence or sexual revictimization, and ultimately places the next generation of females at considerable risk for victimization. (p. 456)

The hows and whys of this finding are more nebulous. If we look only at substance abuse, it has been found that girls and young women who use drugs or alcohol often are likelier to engage in risky sexual behavior than those who do not (CASA 2003). Relevant also is the above discussion concerning the interference of CSA in healthy development of self-concept and "normal" identity growth (Murthi, Servaty-Seib, & Elliott 2006). Finkelhor and Browne (1985) suggested that there are four possible responses to CSA that can raise the likelihood of revictimization: traumatic sexualization, betrayal, powerlessness, and stigmatization. Briere's (2002) self-trauma model suggests that a history of early and severe maltreatment interrupts normal child development and interferes with the acquisition of coping skills related to affect regulation. This "places the individual at risk for being more easily overwhelmed by emotional distress associated with memories of the abuse or trauma, thereby motivating the use of dissociation and other methods of avoidance in adolescence and adulthood" (Briere 2002, p. 185). Maladaptive coping and distorted belief systems can become part of the psychological framework developed from CSA, heightening vulnerability to further revictimization.

In keeping with the idea of "complex personhood" (Gordon 1997), it is essential to note that sexual victimization does not immutably instill dysfunctional identity constructs; instead, survivors actively negotiate and grapple with meanings of the self. For instance, contradictory meanings of female embodiment become even more complicated: the construction of the body as pornified sexual object is the only thing that gets attention, eclipsing personality or character traits, while at the same time the body is the source of degradation and exploitation. Schaffner (2006) finds that "early sexual assault can result in a sexualization of girls' awareness, their psyche, and may force a premature introduction to a sexual sensibility, giving girls a sexualized lens through which they begin to view other sexual interactions" (p. 61). There is a honed sense of the exchange value of the sexualized body, and contradictory feelings of powerlessness and empowerment are derived from this awareness. This has been illustrated by the words of the women I interviewed and is further evidenced in one case study of incest detailed by Russell (1995). She describes the ways that the raping of "Lara" by her grandfather during the majority of her childhood trained her to be sexually provocative and an available object of desire for men. At the same time, she also learned that she could manipulate men (and thus gain a sense of power over them) because of their desire for her body. Lara had multiple self-destructive sexual affairs in which she replayed the conflicts of power from her incest.

In addition to acknowledging the complex emotional terrain that is navigated by sexual violence survivors, it is important to challenge the unbroken and repetitive cycle concept inherent in many portrayals of revictimization. In a meta-analysis of existing research about the effects of child sexual abuse, Paolucci, Genuis, and Violato (2001) found consistency across several outcomes. They found that CSA was associated with PTSD, depression, suicide, sexual promiscuity, and poor academic performance. They also noted that the "victim-perpetrator cycle" was common across existing scholarship on the topic. This concept is not a new one, and perhaps most well known along these lines is Widom's "cycle of violence" theory. Widom first investigated the juvenile and adult criminal records of more than 1,500 individuals to determine the relationship between childhood victimization and adulthood offending. She found that those who had been abused or neglected as children were more likely to be arrested as juveniles, as adults, and for a violent crime. Through publications that disseminated these findings (see Widom 1989a, 1989b, 1989c, 1992), she built and expanded upon her cycle of violence theory. Widom's work has also been roundly criticized, however. Belknap (2007) notes that many of the statistics derived from Widom's research do not distinguish between men and women. It has also been pointed out that directly linking childhood victimization with adult victimization or perpetration is overly simplistic. This critique is in part due to the overemphasis on the individual at the expense of context, particularly in terms of structural conditions that may affect a host of other factors. Ferraro (2006) states,

> That is, the application of cycle models to human experience presumes that there are clear-cut boundaries around experience that allow people to categorize life events so accurately that they can be counted and correlated statistically with other events. . . . People's childhood experiences with abuse influence their adult behaviors, often in destructive ways. But extracting specific abuse events from the larger context of people's lives hides the links between individuals and their social contexts. (pp. 112–113)

Corroborating Ferraro's (2006) argument above, I interrogated the cycle of violence theory by researching how those "within" the cycle became aware of and attempted to disrupt it (Wesely & Wright 2009). Through this approach we intended to problematize the concept of cyclical violence. Based on the qualitative interviews with homeless women, we found that despite experiencing severe violence in childhood and with very few resources at their disposal, the women attempted to disrupt the cycle of violence "from the inside out" by making decisions to actively resist or avoid victimization or perpetration in adulthood. They did *not* unthinkingly or passively reproduce experiences from their past. Their struggles demonstrated that turning recognition into action was problematic when social exclusion, lack of resources, and desperate conditions left the women with few strategies for lasting change. In essence, their efforts succeeded to the extent that it was possible while receiving little to no support. This again speaks to the shortsightedness of focusing only on individuals, since solitary struggles of homeless women occur amid larger oppressive and interlocking inequities that curtail the effectiveness of personal efforts to affect change. Individual lives do not occur in a vacuum, but instead are located within larger social contexts.

Indeed, as noted in Chapter 3, context situates experiences along the continuum of sexualization, and these experiences include both sexual violence and its effects, with impact being mitigated or exacerbated by myriad social factors and conditions. Miller (2008) found that among the urban African American girls with whom she spoke, sexual violence against them—either by boys their age or adult men—was more often than not minimized, ignored, or blamed on the girls. Neighborhood norms discouraged residents from getting involved or speaking to police. Sexual conquest, even by coercion or force, enhanced status among male peer groups. The adherence to this type of masculine construct is something that researchers have found to be heightened in urban disadvantaged communities, and it contributes to the fact that girls' interpretations of sexual violence are discounted, as "many youths defined the girls themselves as sexual agents in these encounters and blamed them for their victimization" (2008, p. 59). Girls in Miller's study reported extremely high rates of sexual harassment and attack, which were "an extension of the broader sexualized treatment young women experienced" in these areas (p. 57). In an environment where sexual violence against girls and women was trivialized or blamed on the victim, where police were not trusted and official intervention was minimal, girls who experienced sexual violence had few resources or support available. This context of urban, racialized poverty thus severely prescribed potentials to heal or recover. Although there are many individual effects of sexual violence, Miller (2008) points out that "in the case of young women in our sample, repeat victimization was particularly likely because they were living in high-crime neighborhoods where groups of adolescent boys and men often congregated unsupervised in public spaces. Thus, part of the risk for repeat victimization resulted from heightened exposure to potential victimizers" (p. 118). In this way, a context of multiple marginalizations conspired against girls' abilities to be protected from sexual violence or its consequences.

When being a victim of child sexual abuse does increase the risk for more sexual victimization, it can also be because it raises the likelihood that girls will run away and seek early independence, creating additional vulnerabilities to exploitation and sexual victimization as they try to survive on their own. As discussed above, early sexual victimization and running away lead to a pattern called "risk amplification" (Chen et al. 2004, p. 1). Bloom et al. (2003) find that sexual, physical, and emotional abuse are significant factors in risky and delinquent behavior among girls and young women. "This effect is long-lasting and creates problems with running away, emotional adjustments, trust and secrecy, future sexuality and other risk behaviors" (p. 127). Though many girls on the streets are running away from home to flee violence, "unlike boys, girls' victimization and their response to that victimization is specifically shaped by their status as young women" (Chesney-Lind & Pasko 2004, p. 27). Being attentive to the relevance of gender includes awareness of how "inequalities between the sexes can differentially affect male and female experiences and behaviors" (Belknap 2007, p. 4). When examining the gendered consequences of running away, studies find that sexually abused female runaways were more likely than either males or nonabused females to have engaged in deviant or delinquent activities such as substance abuse, petty theft, and prostitution (Tyler et al. 2004; McCormack, Janus, & Burgess 1986). "There are few safe options for girls and young women who feel they can no longer live at home" (Bloom et al. 2003, p. 128). Some qualitative research with female prostitutes (Chesney-Lind & Rodriguez 1983; Gilfus 1992; Silbert & Pines 1982) finds that more than half report histories of sexual abuse, many report running away as their first criminal act, and at least one-fourth identify sexual abuse as their reason for becoming prostitutes. Certainly, sex work becomes viable for girls when the survival options are "intricately connected to women's subordinate position in society where victimization by violence [is] coupled with economic marginality" (Gilfus 2006, p. 13). As previously noted, the high risks for further violence while on the streets or surviving through sex work only compound vulnerability and exploitation for this population of young girls.

What is further significant here is that girls who are sexually victimized and escape by running away are criminalized. In comparison to boys, adolescent girls are disproportionately charged with status offenses, which are behaviors that are criminal only when committed by a juvenile (ABA & NBA 2001; United Way of the Bay Area and the San Francisco Juvenile Probation Department 2003). Other status offenses include underage drinking, truancy, and curfew violation (United Way of the Bay Area and the San Francisco Juvenile Probation Department 2003). Girls in this position are then categorized as delinquent and shunted into the juvenile justice system, beginning their entanglement with this institution. For instance, in 1999, girls were only 27 percent of the juveniles arrested overall but accounted for 59 percent of arrests for running away (ABA & NBA 2001).

> Many delinquent girls have been traumatized by sexual and physical abuse, as well as familial substance abuse and domestic violence. Girls often use drugs and alcohol to numb the pain of their childhood trauma. Girls who are victims of sexual abuse are more likely to run away, and girls are more likely than boys to be arrested and ultimately placed outside the home for this behavior.

> Depression is common but often not diagnosed in delinquent girls.
> (ABA & NBA 2001, p. 10)

In Schaffner's (2006) study, she found that girls in juvenile detention recalled being sexualized in relationships with adult men, including their mothers' boyfriends, their fathers, and their stepfathers as well as experiencing sexual degradation by both strangers and close males in their lives. Their unhealed childhood injuries from sexual trauma led to a range of unhealthy consequences, including drugs, alcohol, aggression, and other sexually victimizing scenarios. Further, structural contexts of inequalities shape these outcomes. Racism plays a major role in how girls are labeled and treated in the system, and girls and women of color are disproportionately represented in both the juvenile justice and adult criminal justice systems. As Schaffner (2006) notes, "To talk about girls who are locked up is to talk about racism and race relations in the United States" (p. 49). The imbalance of race and ethnicity within the justice systems has been identified as a key problem by the Department of Justice's Office of Juvenile Justice and Delinquency Prevention. Poverty and low socioeconomic status also have significant impact. Schaffner (2006) reiterates that although girls of all backgrounds face risks of sexual abuse ("well-off girls got molested and ran away too," p. 64), the reality is that "all young women face the possibility of being harmed in childhood, but poor girls face as well the brunt of poverty; lack of adult attention because of overwork, ill health, and disability; untreated substance dependence, death and incarceration of their parents/caregivers; and lack of protection from other harsh conditions such as inadequate health care and unsafe environments" (p. 64).

Beyond running away, survival strategies for girls in these desperate conditions are also criminalized. The 2004 documentary *Girl Trouble* (Leban & Szajko) follows for four years the lives of three at-risk girls who came through the Center for Young Women's Development in San Francisco. The experiences of Stephanie, Sheila, and Shangra mirror the realities described here. All three grew up in conditions of poverty and abuse and entered the system at young teen ages (13, 14, and 16, respectively) for status or nonviolent offenses such as trespassing, running away, and drug possession. This led to a spiraling entrenchment in the juvenile justice system, where punishment did little to alleviate the root causes of their delinquency. The film emphasized that "if we ignore kids who are abandoned, they commit crimes in order to survive, and then the system punishes them." If they fail to meet the conditions of their probation, girls are eligible to be placed in a group home, from which they run away and are forced once again to commit survival crimes on the streets such as drugs and prostitution. "She is [then] labeled as a repeat juvenile offender and will receive increasingly severe sanctions for future violations of the conditions of her court-ordered probation . . . many probation violators report their first offense was actually a status offense" (United Way of the Bay Area and the San Francisco Juvenile Probation Department 2003). Though girls were 27 percent of juveniles arrested in 1999, as noted above, they were also 54 percent of juvenile arrests for prostitution (ABA & NBA 2001). The overlap of victimization and criminalization here is uniquely gendered—it is "criminalized victimization" (Chesney-Lind 2002).

> The tragedy here is that a girl who runs from physical and sexual abuse is forced to confront terrible choices since she does not want to return to an intolerable home, yet she cannot legally go to school, get employment, or find housing without risking return; in short, her legal options are criminalized by a system that has traditionally encouraged her to return home and obey her parents. . . . Faced with terrible choices, some girls turn to survival sex . . . or even some other form of sex work like prostitution. (Chesney-Lind & Irwin 2008, p. 85)

Offending behaviors such as running away and sex work cannot be separated from the gendered context in which they are situated. Running away from home and prostitution are the only two categories in which girls are arrested more often than boys (Belknap 2007; Chesney-Lind & Irwin 2008), and this is no coincidence, especially given the rates of sexual abuse against girls. Adult women are overwhelmingly incarcerated for nonviolent offenses, including the violation of laws that prohibit the sale and possession of specific drugs. Female victims of sexual abuse have the highest rates of drug- and alcohol-related crimes (Chesney-Lind 1997; Daly 1994; Gilfus 1992). Some find that "this pattern of illegal behavior is decidedly gender related—that drug sales and other nonviolent crimes are 'survival crimes' that women commit to earn money, feed a drug-dependent habit, or escape terrifying intimate relationships and brutal social conditions" (Richie 2000, p. 7). Though "not all victims of childhood sexual abuse turn to drugs or crime, sexually victimized children have been found to be three times more apt to become addicted to drugs than nonabused children, and they are also more likely to perpetrate crime, violence and abuse" (Raphael 2007, p. 133)—more evidence of "criminalized victimization."

A finding from Uniform Crime Reports (UCR) states that in 2005 about 18 percent of all violent index crime arrests were of females (US Department of Justice 2005). Raphael (2007) points out that only 20 percent of women in state prison, 12 percent in jails, and 7 percent in federal prison in 2004 had committed violent offenses, with property, drug, and public order crimes making up the rest. For juveniles, "nationally there are a small number of girls arrested for serious violent offenses, such as robbery, homicide and weapon offenses. The crimes are reportedly committed almost exclusively within the context of their relationships with their co-defendants, such as boyfriends or peer group" (United Way of the Bay Area and the San Francisco Juvenile Probation Department 2003, p. 11). Female offending framed as traditionally "male" (e.g., physical violence) is located within gendered contexts. To untangle this, it is useful to engage the pathways perspective, which recognizes that "girls' crimes are usually grounded heavily in the social conditions of their lives and their roles as females within a patriarchal society" (Gaarder & Belknap 2002, p. 485). For example, through gender socialization and other outlets, patriarchy reproduces notions of women's pornified sexualization, which manifest both in girls' self-concepts and in their oppression. These social constructions affect the ways that girls and women may be treated and (de)valued as well as the coping and survival strategies they utilize. In their analysis of two qualitative studies, the first based on ten young women involved in street robbery (Miller 1998) and the second on forty-eight young women in street gangs (Miller & Brunson 2000; Miller & Decker 2001), Miller and White (2004) assert that girls' violence is "produced within social contexts of extreme gender inequality" (p. 187). The authors find that the girls from their studies had to negotiate gendered power imbalances and stereotypes of weakness and sexual availability. Offensive violence was a counteractive measure, a practical choice made while "taking into account the gendered nature of their environments" (p. 186). Though gang membership is a low-level concern for girls,

> as with girls in the juvenile justice system, many gang-involved girls come from homes with a high incidence of sexual abuse,

> domestic violence and family dysfunction. Growing up in poverty, isolated from the economic mainstream, marginalized because of race, class and academic failure, girls most likely to affiliate with gangs tend to feel hopeless about their future. Gang membership puts girls at increased risk of victimization and violence. Girls are treated as sexual property, may be beaten, sexually exploited, sexually assaulted or gang raped. As gang members, they have increased risks of unsafe sex, sexual abuse, teen pregnancy, substance abuse and suicide. (United Way of the Bay Area and the San Francisco Juvenile Probation Department 2003, p. 11)

The criminalization of the behavior of girls and women must take into account how their experiences have been affected along the continuum of sexualization.

Elsewhere I have argued that women's violence should be examined from within a context of cumulative victimization (Wesely 2006). Investigations of women's perpetration of violence historically have not done justice to the complexity of factors from which it arises. Gender socialization naturalizes men's violence, teaching us all that it is an acceptable and even encouraged part of masculinity (Messerschmidt 1993). In contrast, aggression is not traditionally seen as a natural or normal feminine trait. Since female gender roles, socialization patterns, and institutions forbid women's expressions of violence, it "must be viewed as emerging from more intricate motivations" than that of men (Dasgupta 2001, p. 4). Preservation of the binary opposition between masculinity and femininity does little to allow for more nuanced interpretations of women's violence that might provide greater insight. When other structural contexts of inequality (racism; poverty; social exclusion; lack of education, resources, and social services) combine with sexualization and abuse, productive life choices for girls and women are drastically narrowed:

> To understand girls' violence, one must include both a psychosocial framing of adolescence and a critical understanding of connections among patriarchy, racism and poverty. When we broaden the contexts in which we see girls' violent acts occurring to include the realities of the lives of young women, such as their chronic and severe exposure to sexual abuse, sexual harassment, and misogynistic girl hating, we deepen our understanding of their perpetration of violence and can analyze the link between girls' vulnerable social position—unprotected by adult intervention or material advantage—and girls' aggression. Given the moral horizons of gendered opportunities from which urban disadvantaged girls have to

"choose," their choices, while not always legal, make social sense. (Schaffner 2006, p. 132)

As choices are whittled down, girls in desperate environments struggle to avoid further exploitation, feel safe, and survive. Episodes of victimization they endure in such situations are not isolated events but instead a pervasive atmosphere, a chronic condition. A life steeped in violence and exploitation yields desperate girls trying to fight for survival. From within this place of social, institutional, and individual marginalization, violence can emerge as an option.

I have discussed how sexual abuse and exploitation in the young years of a girl's life can heighten her risk of further victimization as well as perpetration, and the social context of her circumstances and environment play a major role in the level of this risk. For those who turn to illegal activities as part of survival or coping—most frequently running away, sex work, and substance abuse—their victimization morphs into criminalization. Compounding the injuries of victimization, when girls are arrested for these crimes, they become a part of the behemoth that is the criminal justice system. Any opportunities to reroute their lives become dramatically reduced at the point they enter the system. This is especially disturbing since the criminal justice system does little to protect these girls while victims but harshly apprehends them when they offend. "The crime processing system, which has historically failed to respond to incest victims and other child abuse victimizations in the home, has diligently responded to girls who have run away from home or committed other offenses" (Belknap 2007, p. 109). If there was any question as to the level of victimization girls who offend had experienced, we only need to examine the proportion of incarcerated women who report CSA. The US Department of Justice (Harlow 1999) found that in 1999 57 percent of women in state prison, 40 percent in federal facilities, 48 percent in jail, and 40 percent of female probationers had been victimized physically or sexually before incarceration (compared to 16 percent, 7 percent, 13 percent, and 9 percent of men, respectively). Thirty-nine percent of state women prisoners and 37 percent of female jail detainees had been sexually abused specifically, and almost 26 percent of all female state prisoners were molested before the age of 18. Raphael (2007) notes that research at specific jails and prisons reveals even higher percentages, with a 1999 study at a New York facility—Bedford Hills Maximum Security Correctional

Facility—finding that 59 percent of the women experienced some form of sexual abuse during childhood or adolescence. Ferraro (2006) finds that official data show that about 60 percent of incarcerated women have experienced abuse, but that qualitative studies and estimates reveal even higher numbers—from 75 to 90 percent. Fagan (2001) compiled existing qualitative and quantitative findings and notes that a majority of female offenders report histories of abuse "occurring over a long period of time and by multiple offenders" (p. 457). From qualitative interviews with female incarcerated offenders, she finds that 63 percent were sexually abused (derived from Chesney-Lind & Rodriguez 1983), and from qualitative interviews with female incarcerated street offenders, that 75 percent were sexually abused (derived from Gilfus 1992). Secondary effects from traumatic abuses linger while girls and women are locked up. Among one sample of incarcerated youth, girls were 50 percent more likely to be suffering from PTSD than the equivalent male population (Steiner, Garcia, & Mathews 1997).

Interplay Along the Continuum of Sexualization

This chapter has demonstrated the range of effects that can result from individual experiences along the continuum of sexualization. From pornified sexualization to sexual abuse and all the areas in between, we see that girls in our society are growing up at high risk for psychological, emotional, and physical damage. The full severity of their destruction will only become apparent as we raise another generation of girls in this increasingly harsh climate. Along the continuum, there is also interplay within. Pornified sexualization impacts sexual violence, and sexual violence reinforces and reflects the objectification and dehumanization inherent in these constructs of girls and women. Of course, these effects are not prepackaged. This chapter has pointed out that a consequence of any experience along the continuum may be exacerbated or mitigated by a range of factors, the most important of which are the structural context and the social conditions this context generates. In the next chapter, effects and context will be examined in greater depth through a detailed return to the two case studies.

5
Tracing Pathways to Victimization

I wanted a change and I had to have something tangible happen in my life and I knew, I said lord, if you can hear me, change me. Bring me something into my life, or just take me because I'm tired. I was just tired. I was tired of paying my rent and men coming in, just taking my body. I was tired of being tired and I was sick of being sick. And I was tired of the life that I was living and I knew my children were growing up and I didn't want them to see me like this. I don't want to turn into my mother and father. —*Eliza, age 45*

In this chapter, I add greater dimension to the discussion from the previous chapter about effects of the continuum of sexualization. In Chapter 3, I focused on the two case studies with populations of exotic dancers and homeless women to explore the ways that context can situate initial experiences along the continuum of sexualization. Individuals in these two groups were multiply marginalized, and this structured the conditions of their lives, in many ways increasing their risks along the continuum. Chapter 4 went on to explicate the general range of consequences that can result from experiences along the continuum of sexualization for girls and women across the board. Here, then, the foci of Chapters 3 and 4 come together in an investigation of context and consequences. I examine in depth the case studies of women I discuss throughout this book, looking at how context structured their paths and the outcomes from their experiences along the continuum of sexualization. In particular, I examine effects in terms of their dreams and goals, decisions, further victimization, and even perpetration as they became adults. The case studies of exotic dancers and homeless women provide two illustrations of how consequences of experiences along the continuum of sexualization are contextualized within particular structural conditions and institutional arrangements. Those in the case studies I examine have choices and options constrained by many inequalities, but their experiences are examples of the depth at which girls and women can be impacted by the continuum without any advantages to protect them. Unlike Chapter 3, in which I separated the case studies, in this chapter I arrange sections by life events and choices as the women entered adulthood. This is an effective organization of the women's narratives and most powerfully demonstrates the effects of the continuum.

Relationship and Family Ideals

The women's narratives in Chapter 3 reflected childhood lived experiences along a continuum of sexualization that ranged from degradation to victimization. These experiences were rooted in larger contexts of structural disadvantage, especially in terms of economic hardship and social exclusion. Chapter 3 culminated with early independence, homelessness, and other risky survival options being identified as preferable to victimization experiences along the continuum while still in the childhood home. This reality often exposed the women to the potential for more victimization as they moved into adulthood.

For most, including those who turned to a life on the streets (by running away or otherwise leaving home permanently during adolescence), the dream of being loved became paramount. Ruby, for instance, fantasized about being a part of a different family: "I didn't want to live at home no more. I didn't want to—to be honest, when I was growing up I didn't want my own family. I didn't want to be a part of my family. I wanted to be in somebody else's family. To be happy. Because there was no love." Ferraro (2006) draws on in-depth interviews with forty-five criminally offending women and finds that almost all of them married or became "intimately involved with men as a way out of their parents' homes" (p. 131). More specifically, as Ferraro (2006) noted, "It was often an experience of sexual abuse or assault, at home or by a stranger, that preceded a young woman's pregnancy and decision to leave home" (p. 132). Sara, who left home at 15 because she was "tired of being a punching bag," looked for someone to love her, as her family had not. She had her first child at 15 and six more by the age of 25, when I interviewed her. For the past eight years (since she was 17) she had been involved with an extremely abusive man. She says, "I guess I was trying to get affection from anywhere I could, because I wasn't getting it from my father or my parents. So I guess when the other two guys showed me affection, I just kinda clinged to it." Though they longed for love and affection in intimate relationships, there was not much of a blueprint to follow. Tamara, for instance, recalled that male abuse during most of her young life was the norm: "I had watched [my father] beat my mother with a belt just like he beat us. . . . All my life seeing my father beat my mother with a belt, [and] my sister's abusive husband that raped me and beat me."

Whether or not the household was rife with abuse, these homes were nonetheless typically characterized by the "empty families" I described earlier, a term used by Schaffner (2006) in her research. In empty families, there is neglect or chaos rather than security or stability. Children's needs are unidentified or unmet because of the problems of the parent or parents and their crises with employment, money, substances, the criminal justice system, illness, social exclusion, and loss. Not only are adults in these empty families often sporadically absent in the physical sense, but they are emotionally unavailable as they try to cope with the monumental obstacles to their own daily survival. In addition to the fact that this leaves children without guidance or protection, it can result in the "parentified child—someone who takes care of everyone else in the family, doing parenting work, often for her own parents, often for younger siblings" (Schaffner 2006, p. 96). I saw parentification repeatedly among the childhood descriptions of the women I interviewed—girls who tried to take on the economic responsibilities of the family, who raised younger siblings, who cared for a depressed or substance-influenced parent. Tasha and Rita were two women who began exotic dancing when there were no more resources at home. In Tasha's case, as mentioned previously, the electricity was turned off in the house she shared with her mother, and she felt she had no other choice. Others took on adult responsibilities in different ways. Eliza said, "And so, when my mother would be on her drunk binge, I would try to go in the house and clean the house. I would find a little bar of soap and I would wash the dishes and clean up the house and kind of set it in place." Ruby describes a similar situation: "I took my mom through the whole phase of drinking. I was always there. Always babied her. Always cleaned her up. Always put her in the bed and I be the main one she beat on." Dee, who would console her mother when she cried, explained, "I guess I grew up too quick. I don't think I had a teenage-hood."

Because of such sentiments and experiences, most of the women in this study were highly motivated to have a different life and, initially, confident in their abilities to move on. Eliza says, "I just always knew—there was something in me that knew this way was dysfunctional. This is not the life I want. This is not the life I want for my children. And it's not how I wanted to live." This is echoed by the words of Cammie, who married at age 18: "I had it in my head that I was going to show everybody in my family, especially my parents, that you could have a marriage and make it work, you can have children and you can have a family and you can do it right." Richie (1996) conducted qualitative life history interviews with thirty-seven women incarcerated at the Rose M. Singer Center at Rikers Island Correctional Facility in New York City, focusing on the narratives of African American battered women. She found that although the women's families were not consistent with the ideological ideal, they remained highly influenced by this social imperative, as evidenced by their "dreams about marriage and family life [and] their role models" (p. 56). Richie (1996) noted that all of the women in her study initially desired the traditional, heterosexual nuclear family. "For the women whose lives were characterized by extreme poverty or sexual abuse, ideologically normal families were considered a potential way out of their despair" (p. 135). Many in her study felt their families of origin "afforded them the emotional and material opportunity to imagine something different for their futures," and others saw "the establishment of a traditional family structure as a way to escape their troubled homes" (p. 136). Other qualitative research on similar populations has found that women who grow up in empty families and amid the chaotic environs of extreme poverty and violence often put major efforts into attaining the ideologically normal, nuclear family (Ferraro 2006; Raphael 2000).

"Doing it right" is difficult, however, from within such a disadvantaged context. Ruby says, "All my relationships were very abusive and that's what I thought love was about. I didn't know no better. Any time they would beat me up and—they would beat me up bad and they would tell me later on they loved me. And I'd say, OK. And keep going and going and going that way. And that's like I learned." When these relationships became violent, "the physical and emotional abuse so deeply contradicted the women's expectations that they initially deny the seriousness and rationalize the abuse, ultimately finding themselves isolated and in very dangerous situations" (Raphael 2000, p. 17). For instance, Junie says, "I thought, my God, he just loves me so much, I can't talk to anyone, I can't go anywhere. I don't know if it was because I saw my mother go through it. For some reason you start to think, oh, they just really love you and they don't want you to go anywhere." The power and control implicit in the abuser's treatment of Junie is not seen for what it is—her deep desire for a "normal" relationship along with her past experiences frames her partner's behaviors as loving ones.

As hopes for a better life dwindled and the burdens of abusive relationships and unstable living conditions bound them more tightly, the women became increasingly mired in damaging circumstances for which there seemed few alternatives. Eliza recalls, "I only wanted to be a nurse and wife and raise children and live in a normal house, a normal life. And that didn't come." Why was it so hard for the hopes to mesh with reality for women such as Eliza? One theory is that severe childhood experiences along the continuum of sexualization replaced words and dialogue with violence: "The ever-present fear of violence prevents children from developing capabilities for hearing and knowing. . . . Because of its unpredictable nature, violence interferes with this necessary sense of an ordered world, essential for the development of healthy children" (Raphael 2000, p. 19). The abusive childhoods experienced by the women were contexts in which the development of emotional and intellectual skills necessary for successful relationships was absent or disordered. As discussed in Chapter 4, sexual abuse, in particular, challenges the healthy development of boundaries and self-protection for girls. The feelings and experiences of each individual are then located within and intersect with social inequalities and dynamics of power. Ferraro (2006) pulls together a textured analysis that fleshes out the complexity of these intersections as she introduces a chapter called "The Social Reproduction of Women's Pain":

> I argue that the emotional and physical pain inflicted by family members on children and adults is deeply embedded in complex

> structures of feeling that are linked to larger social contexts. . . . When daughters feel lonely and unloved and as young women are "swept off their feet" by a violent, abusive man, they align with structures of feeling about romance, masculine power, and overwhelming passion. They are not simply making bad choices or replicating the behavior of their parents. . . . People's needs for recognition, meaning and connection to others are channeled and restricted by larger social structures, particularly economic and labor structures. The social control of desire cuts across race, class, and gender boundaries and is also influenced by these axes of domination. (pp. 108–110)

Despite their best efforts to achieve a "normal" nuclear family, then, complex contexts of disadvantage kept this dream from being realized for many of the women.

Limited Options and Victimization

West (1999) states that "control of one's body and environment are in many respects elusive goals for women in our cultural climate where violations of women are so routine" (p. 178). It was from within this "cultural climate" that the effects of the continuum of sexualization emerged for these women, only to be further constrained by a matrix of disadvantages and abuses. Effects in the form of decisions that they made about their lives then put them, as young adults, at even higher risk for violence and played into the chronic exploitation and victimization they endured. The women were also revictimized by intermittent and ongoing feelings of being unsafe, unprotected, and silenced by both individuals and society at large, perpetrators who experienced few consequences for their actions, and the message that their value as human beings was minimized as violence against them was condoned and justified. These lived experiences, along with the lack of support and the lack of options for the women, maintained these grim realities. As a result, the violent victimizations they experienced were not just isolated events, but a pervasive atmosphere of cumulative violence.

Intimate relationships of the women perpetuated many of the same problems they had already experienced along the continuum of sexualization, such as sexual victimization and exploitation, economic instability, and drug and alcohol addictions. Again, these experiences were located within a structural context of marginalizations and intensified the women's exclusion from social support and resources while reinforcing emotional instability and physical danger. Generally, these lived experiences contributed to a downward spiral in which the women were preoccupied with daily survival, beaten down, depressed, and unsuccessful at making choices or having opportunities that improved their life conditions. Twenty-six of the forty women interviewed (eighteen out of twenty homeless women and eight out of twenty exotic dancers) had been victimized in at least one adult intimate relationship. Seven of the dancers also described being stalked. The immediacy of this violence was driven home when I had an interview with Tracy, who had a split lip and dried blood on her jean jacket. Although she did not admit this to the homeless shelter workers, she confided that her boyfriend stopped by on his bike and she met him outside, where they got in a "fight," at which time she was injured in the mouth.

An extremely disturbing lived experience came from Angel, an 18-year-old exotic dancer, who told of a homicide she witnessed at the hands of her abuser and rapist. The details are gruesome, and her story, like others', continues to haunt me. Angel ran away from home at the age of 15, after becoming close with an 18-year-old woman named Ricki. They met a 27-year-old man, Chris, who convinced the two girls to move in with him and live under his name, becoming their guardian. Initially, of course, Chris seemed "nice." He owned a strip club and had expendable cash, a beach house, and lots of connections he used to impress Angel and Ricki. When Angel turned 16, Chris asked her if she wanted to begin dancing at his club, and she did, while becoming increasingly dependent on him. Along with this dependence, Chris started introducing more and more terror into the girls' lives. Angel's first sexual experience was being raped by Chris while his friends watched. She and Ricki both became pregnant by Chris. After Ricki gave birth to a baby boy and Angel was still pregnant, there was a vicious gang rape attempt by Chris and his friends that resulted in Ricki's death. Angel, a minor, stayed with Chris to raise Ricki's baby for three years and was raped and beaten consistently during this timeframe by Chris and others. Here, Angel's description of the murder in her own words:

> This plays through my mind nonstop, every day. But we were laying there handcuffed together, completely naked, thinking what's going to happen to us, what are they going to do. They were all on

drugs. And that's the only reason I'd never touch drugs in my whole life. [Chris] decided he was going to inject us with heroin to calm us down a little bit. So he held our arms down, and he injected us. And that's the first time I ever had drugs in my body at all, and I had a very violent reaction to it. And I started flipping out right away. And I was pregnant, I was like, what are you doing to my baby? It all happened so fast. This guy started to get on Ricki, and this other guy put his dick in my mouth. And she kneed him, and I bit him, so hard. And they got really really upset about that. I guess if we had just had gone along with it, we would have been fine. But we weren't. He took a crowbar and he just started on Ricki. Just ripping her to pieces. I have never seen so much blood in my life. It was like a movie. He just, I kept looking over at her and just crying my eyes out. Because her head was completely cut off right here. It was . . . she was gone. I thought how can this person take away my only friend in the entire world. It was just. . . . I'm shaking. . . . And she was the sweetest . . . most . . . everything. And she had a month old baby. Who was still breast feeding, still needed his mother. So . . . I was still handcuffed to her, and he took her body and put her in this bag, and took her out to the alley and unhandcuffed us, and I just laid there in this little ball, thinking, I want to die. I thought about suicide for a long time. I didn't know how I could go on, seeing what I'd seen, knowing what I knew. . . . The only thing that kept me alive was her little boy. Because every time I looked at him . . . he had her eyes. He called me mom. I took care of him for 3 years. And then I gave him up for adoption.

The day Angel turned 18 she gave the boy up for adoption and left the state while Chris was at work, making her final escape.

Angel's harrowing experiences are compounded by the fact that there were no consequences, legal or otherwise, for Chris's actions. When I asked about justice for the atrocities committed against her and Ricki, Angel replied, "Legally, no. He knew too many people. I don't know what happened to [Ricki's body]. There was no funeral." She describes,

He got away with it. There were times I would just fly at him with my fists, and think I was ready to kill him. And I'd just get knocked on my ass. The only time I remember that I actually fought back was the time he broke three of my ribs. I saw a doctor that came to the house, 'cause Chris didn't want anybody else to know what he did. . . . He would have a lot of people who would keep his secret. He came off to people as really friendly, and a lot of people he hung out with were drug users. . . . I want him to be caught. Chris has ruined so many people's lives.

Angel's experiences with social and medical services in the traumatic aftermath of tragedy provided her with no support. Chris used his connections to keep his crimes secret. And Angel's social isolation and exclusions did not end there. She was also victimized by law enforcement:

> I really haven't had that much respect for authority and law. There were a couple of police officers one time that came into the club and when I was walking outside they were standing there. And they assaulted me. They touched me, put their hands all over me, both of them. And it was like, who can I turn to? When I can't even trust authority, when the authority is doing this. There were numerous officers that would come over to our house in California that Chris knew. And would, you know, join in [on the rapes], with these people. About once a week or so, for three years, there would be people [who would rape her].

Angel's story typifies revictimization at every turn—interpersonally and then with various social, criminal justice, and legal actors, who not only did not help her but exploited and violated her further. Her narrative about her lived experiences illustrates the structural context in which women can be violently victimized and trapped.

Violent victimization clearly went beyond intimate partner abuse. It occurred in a range of circumstances where lives were circumscribed by a structure of disadvantages and vulnerabilities. Marie noted that, as a dancer, she was offered little protection from victimization:

> He'd try to show off in front of his guy friends and bite you on the rear end. If you got bit in a grocery store, the guy would get prosecuted for that, and go to jail. You do it in a topless bar and it's OK. It's ridiculous. Just because you're in the atmosphere you have permission. It's like when we get bit on the rear, they don't give you counseling for that. But if a police officer came to a case where you

got bit, they would give you a card: here, you can call this counselor, this is a form of victimization or whatever. And you would go to get counseling. But dancing, all these things would happen to you and you don't get one ounce of counseling. You're just getting victimized left and right. And they don't treat it as victimization, they treat it as, oh, it comes with the territory. They don't tell you that when you're getting hired! They don't tell you, oh, you can get bit, get slapped, men call you names, men can spit on you. They don't tell you those things.

The level of risk and lack of consequences for offensive acts are heightened for exploited and devalued populations such as the homeless and sex workers. Gina met a customer while working as a dancer and went on several dates with him. She was raped in her own home by the man, and she describes, "Many times I tried to struggle against him, like no, I don't want this, come on, stop kissing me. And eventually I just gave up. I was like, alright, fine, whatever, do your job. I knew I was just a cheap little piece of ass to him."

Like the dancers, many of the homeless women described constantly defending themselves from propositions and attacks—both from homeless men and from men driving past them on the street. Women's assessments of vulnerability and fear related to sexual victimization are incorporated into identity and guide daily behaviors. Hollander (2001) finds that "women report constantly monitoring their environment for signs of danger, hesitating to venture outside alone or even in the company of other women, asking men for protection, modifying their clothes . . . and restricting their activities. . . . These strategies are simply part of daily life as a woman" (p. 105). The "daily lives" of at-risk women, like those on the street, make it difficult for them to assuage their fears—let alone reduce their risk of victimization—using these techniques. As Tamara states,

> By being a woman—a homeless woman that's on the street, it's dangerous. You have homeless men, and it's co-ed when you're sleeping on the street. It's co-ed and some of them approach women that want women to give them favors sexually. Too, sometimes, they get bold enough, they try to rape the women, and a lot of homeless women do be raped. Raped and murdered. They will murder them in the alleyways and you will find homeless women in the dumpster. Someone slit her throat. . . . Always, the homeless women are being

approached in the street by homeless men that want to have sex with them, oral sex with them. Some of them offer them money and some of them don't offer them anything, or tell them they'll beat them up if they don't. And most of the homeless women are scared, and they'll go ahead and do it. . . . Mostly homeless women that don't have checks monthly, how they make their money is tricking to regular men that have families, wives and children. They park on the corners; they meet them at certain times, and these are homeless women. That's how they survive. They do that as we speak.

From Tamara's statement we get the sense that homeless women may be, literally, scared into sex; sex then becomes a strategy for negotiating the streets, if not surviving them.

For the women discussed here, severe experiences along the continuum of sexualization throughout their lives amplified the messages that all women receive about their bodies. For some, the sexualized body was further reduced to an object when it became their only tool for survival. Tracy worked as a prostitute for twenty-seven years:

You don't have feelings when you are messing with a client—a trick. So I don't trip with that. When he gets up on top of me, I just say, OK, what am I going to do with this man's money, now. That's what I do. I've been shot, raped, kidnapped. I was sodomized, the whole nine yards. From tricks. Pulled a gun. . . . I can't let my head think about the things that I've been through.

Tracy seems to distance or even disassociate from her body in order to cope, a response also found among survivors of childhood sexual abuse (Barnett, Miller-Perrin, & Perrin 2005). Others engaged in sex for survival on the streets and struggled with identity meanings in different ways. As Marion describes it:

Well, I remember one time while I was homeless I was walking down the street crying. I was crying—it was late at night and I was tired and I was scared because it was like a weekend and there was a lot of people on the street. And they was looking at me and I was scared and this guy stopped. And he said, "Are you OK?" And I told him no and he said "Why?" I told him that I stunk so bad that people thought I was a dope addict and I'm not, I was just homeless and he said, "Well, you could come to my house and take a shower" and he said "I won't bother you." And he was a young good-looking guy and I told him OK, you know? So he took me to his place—he said I couldn't spend the night because he had roommates. You know, but he would give me—he said he had some clean clothes and I could take a shower. And he would give me something to eat. So I got—he gave his word. . . . He got in the shower. He got in the shower with me. I had sex with him. When I got in the shower, he got in the shower with me and he was kind of attractive, so I didn't mind.

When I asked her, "Do you feel like you had sex with him in exchange for these things [i.e., clothes, food, shower]?" Marion seems unsure, replying, "No, he made me feel—I guess he made me feel that I had sex with him because I wanted to have sex with him." Marion does not narrate the event as one of straightforward sexual exchange. Her fluid framing of this event—in which the man capitalized on his position of offering the basic necessities of food, shower, and clothing that Marion needed—illustrates her struggle to contextualize the use of her sexualized body for survival without relinquishing a sense of agency. It exemplifies the "sexual solution to a nonsexual problem" that so often typified reality from an early age for women in these highly disadvantaged social, economic, and cultural positions. This also repeats an earlier paradox—that the sexually objectified body plays a dominant role in female identity and value even as it is a source of degradation and exploitation.

Rena, who had one of the most extensive histories of sexual abuse and rape through her childhood, teenage, and adult years, perceived her survival on the streets as something based in defensive strategies to avoid being targeted for sexual attack. She describes, "I'd just sit up all night. Every time. Every single time. Sit straight up. That's right. Tired as hell and just sit up." When Rena arrived at the shelter where I interviewed her, she explained this decision by drawing upon the impacts of her previous sexual victimization:

I was lucky I didn't get raped recently. And a friend of mine say, man, what are you doing? Get up. Come inside. I was on a damn sidewalk. That's why I'm here [at the shelter] in a way, because when I left from that crack house [where raped] I came right here. . . . And just go ahead on and quit being—bite my pride. Because I never thought the day [would come] I'd have to come here, but look where I'm at. Because I'd rather be up here than to be out there, somebody sticking their dick in my mouth or in my vagina or in my whatever you want to call it or just taking advantage of me. Really, I say, oh well, let's go, bite your tongue, let's go. Here I am. Sometimes you have to let your pride go. And I'm going, I'm not ashamed of it. I say, it beats prostituting. I'm not out prostituting to stay with anybody. I'm not out, you know, doing whatever. I'm here.

Rena's statement also reflects the gendered lesson that women on the street have two options: be raped, or "voluntarily" use sex in exchange for money, food, or safety. These examples are all connected to the complex context that situates the continuum of sexualization for these women.

Institutions such as the criminal justice system, designed to protect, unfortunately fell short of meeting the women's safety needs, reinforcing structural arrangements of gender inequality. This is evident in earlier examples, like that of Angel. Cammie provides another instance when she described a punitive rather than palliative reaction after calling the police on an abusive partner:

The last time I called the police on him just before I left my house, the police officer said, "We checked the record before we came here. In the last 30 days, you've called us 15 times. If we have to come back out here again, somebody is going to jail." Because [my husband] used to—when we'd get to the point where I would call the police, he would take off. So he wouldn't be there for them to lock him up. This is what they were saying to me: "The next time we come out here, somebody's going to jail. Even if it's you." And I mean, I got kind of mouthy with them. I said, "You're gonna take me to jail, for what? For calling the law, you know?"

Such negative responses from law enforcement heightened vulnerabilities for the women by restricting their choices. Sara says of her husband, "I left because he was continuously smoking crack cocaine and he was beating on me. And moving away from him and in with a friend, but he kept my son and the police wouldn't allow me to take my son, because there's no custody papers. So eventually I went back for the simple fact of my child being there." That was the first time

Sara tried to leave her abuser. The second time, she faced the same barriers with the police:

> I left him a second time when I had four children by him. He had threatened to kill me. I tried to take my kids out of the house and he wouldn't let me. I called the cops, told the cops that he was abusive and he had a history of it and I just wanted to go over there and get my stuff and my children and again they told me I couldn't take my kids if he didn't allow it and of course, he didn't.

Sara ended up being transient with her abuser and children, staying with family and then a hotel. When her kids were removed from her care, she says, "I was just tired of everything and I had reached my limit with him. . . . And that night he threatened to kill me. He said he'd already lost his kids, he wasn't about to lose me, and that was just it for me." At that point Sara left and went to a homeless shelter and thus began her episodes of homelessness as she struggled to stabilize her life.

Molly was raped at an extended-stay hotel catering to low-income individuals. Male attackers broke the chain off the door. She says, "I felt vulnerable when they came in and used my body the way they did. You know. I'm not safe here. What I did was sort of like put booby traps up to my door so it would wake me up if anybody would come in my room." When Molly reported the rape at the extended stay hotel, police were ineffectual. She says, "Honey, what could I do except call the police for help? But they never really helped much." Already multiply marginalized, the women often described resentment toward law enforcement's apparent indifference to the protection of stigmatized populations of women. After being raped in a "crack house," Rena contacted the police. She describes it as follows:

> So anyway, I wakes up with the guy on top of me, on top of me with the knife on my throat. And my menstrual was on—and the guy did what he had to do. Blood was everywhere. He didn't even know I was bleeding and I say that's what you get, motherfucker. And I cussed the dude out and I called the cops and the cops didn't do doodley squat. I was outdone. I say OK, if I blow this man's brains out today, or get a knife and stab the hell out of him, just be prepared to take me to 33rd [jail]. Because . . . you know, why they

didn't do anything? Because it was a doggone crack house in a crack area. That's why. So they probably say, yeah, she's probably lying. I don't know what that man told them but when they took the handcuffs off [him] . . . I was too pissed. I say, what the hell good is the police? You know? Really.

The needs of sex workers on the streets and homeless women may be further ignored because they do not fit appropriate, conventional constructions of female identity: "Ideas of femininity and of the proper behavior of a 'good girl' permeate the police, the courts, and the correctional institutions" (Madriz 1997, p. 31). Rena's sense that the police thought she was lying about being raped because she was in a "crack house" reflects the possibility that she was not considered a "good girl" and so not an "appropriate" female victim.

As discussed earlier, sexual and physical victimization are vastly underreported. It is no surprise, then, that the shame and fear derived from being abused kept many of the women from reporting in the first place. In *Hard Lives, Mean Streets* (Jasinski et al. 2010), we show based on quantitative results that although rape was experienced at least once by half of the sample, only 40 percent of those victims reported the crime to police. Reasons for not reporting were typified by the experience of Ruby, who described being tricked into going into an apartment with a female acquaintance paid by her assailant. The woman quickly abandoned Ruby in the apartment, and the attacker threatened Ruby with a knife, sprayed her with Mace until she could not breathe, and forced her to perform oral sex. She never told anyone. When I asked her why she did not report this crime to the police, she responded, "I was ashamed. It was dumb; it was stupid. Following behind someone else . . . if I go to them they [will] say, 'What [were] you doing up there? Why did you go?' and question me. And I don't have no answer for them." Ruby's response indicates that she felt the police would blame her, particularly because, as she said, "it was in a rough neighborhood," which implies she should have known better. This compounded her shame. Richie (1996) found that women also felt shame when their requests for help or assistance were ignored by the system. She said that "some battered women actually feel worse when the services ignore the violence, as this experience *reinforces* their sense of shame, guilt and powerlessness" (p. 141). Such experiences with agencies and institutions such as the criminal justice system reified destructive lessons of sexual victimization for the women and continued to shape their interpretation of their vulnerabilities.

Perpetration

As noted in Chapter 4, the perpetration of violence and other crimes can be an effect of or resistance against experiences along the continuum of sexualization for girls and women. This is consistent with the behaviors of some of the women I interviewed who did act as perpetrators of illegal activities. Any discussion of this violence must be rooted in, rather than divorced from, the structural contexts and the desperate realities that shaped their lived experiences. It is helpful to frame the aggression of girls and women broadly, incorporating an understanding of experiences along the continuum of sexualization and their psychosocial effects as well as structural contexts that can include patriarchy, racism, and poverty. Dasgupta (2001) calls for this understanding in her review of the research on women's violence within intimate heterosexual relationships. She notes that studies have pointed at a number of reasons for women's assaultive behavior, but that these still oversimplify the sources of these actions. Suggesting an "ecologically nested" framework, Dasgupta (2001) encourages us to look at the interactions ranging from the individual to the structural and historical, asserting that this is a more comprehensive and accurate lens through which to view women's violence. Within the ecologically nested approach, she also attends to gender, stating that "female gender roles and socialization patterns as well as socio-political institutions historically forbid expressions of aggression against their male partners, [so] women's violence must be viewed as emerging from more intricate motivations" than that of men (2001, p. 4). With this in mind, the ecologically nested approach foregrounds the interviewees' lived experiences along the continuum of sexualization and their structural locations.

Just as it is true for the "choices" participants made, coping and survival strategies from within their lived experiences and social positions are constrained. As mentioned above, even when the women do turn to agencies such as the criminal justice system for relief, the police are seldom seen as a safe or helpful contact and can even act as agents of revictimization and violation. Such reactions from social institutions drive home a reality that the women can depend on no one but themselves for their safety. From within this place of social, institutional, and individual marginalization, violence emerges as an option. Based on extensive literature review, Rumgay (1999) notes that "where female violence reflects a lifestyle choice, that choice is made in the context of deep and chronic social and personal disadvantage" (p. 119). In my two case studies, fully half the exotic dancers reported using violence, with almost the same amount (nine out of twenty) of homeless women acknowledging their perpetration. These findings are similar to Schaffner's (2006) in that "episodes of violent offense cannot be bundled into neat and discrete categories by 'type of girl'" (p. 133). In the more than 100 detained girls in her study, she found that those who acted out violently were white suburban girls, working-class white girls, girls of color, girls who regularly got high, and girls who were clean. We must eschew strict categorization and listen to how anger and aggression are experienced by young women who perpetrate violence.

> Taking their anger and aggression seriously relocates our attention to the structural conditions of their lives—such as growing up amid poverty and sexism—instead of focusing on the individual psychological failures of the girls surviving those conditions. In that context, girls' aggression is seen as a real response to real problems . . . their aggression is in direct relation to their oppressive contexts. (Schaffner 2006, p. 145)

In many ways, the women resist, through violence, the cumulative victimization experienced in their lives.

For example, in an atmosphere of ongoing victimization along the continuum of sexualization, some of the exotic dancers I interviewed described their violent reactions to verbal degradations and physical violations by customers. Irene recalls,

> Oh yeah, guys would say derogatory comments a lot. It's like, as the night wore on, the drunker some of the guys got, the ruder they got. One time this guy stuck his head between my legs—I was standing—and kind of pushed up on it. And I looked at him and I threw a glass, and I got in trouble for throwing the glass. I did hit his head with my hand, but not the glass.

Glass bottles, spiked heels, fists, and slamming customers' heads against the wall were all tools of violent resistance described by the women. Skye actually lost her job for responding this way to a customer.

I get grabbed in the club pretty frequently. I spill a beer on them or kick their ass. I don't think many of them realize just what kind of weapons you wear on your feet. And that spike can be very painful against your penis. And that has happened. I've hit customers. I got fired from one club for hitting a guy. He kissed my butt when I bent over. And I turned around and punched him in the mouth. I got fired for not getting a bouncer.

Skye's solution reflects the belief that staff rarely took dancers' concerns seriously, again emphasizing the larger lesson that the women cannot depend on those who are supposed to protect them. Gina describes punching out a customer who got on stage with her. When I asked her where the bouncer was at the time, she replied, "Probably doing a shot." Marie recalls a man who exposed himself to her repeatedly through a hole in his pants. Management refused to remove him until they observed the exposed penis themselves. Staff contributed to the degradation and violation of the women, capitalizing on contexts of disadvantage that shaped the women's vulnerability to exploitation. Marie had sex with a staff member on stage after closing while the manager watched. She also performed oral sex on a manager, "that he asked me for in his office. The managers totally take advantage of it." Paula's experience was another example of degradation, the lack of protection, and her ensuing violent resistance:

When I was working at X Club, they have what's called a bush dive. It's the way they tip. They're sitting in a chair, and then they have a railing that comes up from the side. So when they tip the girls, they put the dollar in the railing and lean back over that, and the girls come and dance over them. It's nude. And that's when the taking liberties happens. I shoved my spike in a guy's temple. I don't take shit from anybody. And when you're violating my person, MY PERSON, I don't go for that. And I don't see why any woman should have to. Especially when it took fifteen minutes after that just to find a fucking bouncer. They tried to tell me they couldn't do anything because they didn't see it. I'm like, motherfucker, I know you have cameras back there and you better watch them. 'Cause this guy is lifting his head during a bush dive. You ain't going to do that shit with me.

Paula is clearly angry and refuses to "take shit," in this way justifying her violent resistance to being violated. Violent resistance can develop out of these ongoing experiences of vulnerability and exploitation, which create a milieu in which the women had to be vigilant about their own safety.

Irene used violence on at least three different occasions. In one case, she was physically threatened while performing a private dance for a customer and resisted by stabbing him in the leg with an ice pick. She was arrested and then released when her own injuries were revealed. Another time, a male friend who knew she was a dancer insisted on sex, and Irene hit him over the head with a fire extinguisher. In addition, while hitchhiking, the driver of a vehicle attempted to coerce her into sexual interactions. She responded by punching him in the face, chest, and crotch and jumping out of the car. The more Irene was exposed to these terrifying events of attempted sexual attack, the more determined she was to protect herself. She says, "I got a .38, which is small enough to fit in your pocket, and I carried that every night with me, from my car to the club and from the club to my car." The gun is a symbol of her violent resistance. Skye, another exotic dancer, describes being stalked on numerous occasions, raped in her car, and stabbed in a parking lot by a customer. Like Irene, she purchased a gun, and she says, "I'll use it if I have to." Contexts of cumulative victimization along the continuum of sexualization affect life circumstances, which then shape existing, day-to-day realities where the participants violently resist being victimized yet again.

The women's description of their violence also reinforces that they were determined to resist more victimization. Recall Angel, the woman who endured extended periods of horrific violence in addition to witnessing her friend's murder and who was abused and revictimized by law enforcement. Even though she did survive her traumatic ordeal, she was rarely able to successfully resist at that time. After escaping the violent situation, her responses to perceived offenses became what, from the outside, might seem disproportionately severe. Cumulative victimization along the continuum of sexualization affected the way she interprets and reacts to current violations. Now, she says, "I just don't tolerate it anymore." She carries Mace and uses it "constantly," spraying anyone who bothers her.

There's been situations. I walked into a Circle K [convenience store] to get cigarettes, and there was nobody else around, and the cashier said, "What's on your boob?" He's like, [points] right here. I'm like, "That's a mole. Nice come-on, asshole." And I just sprayed him. Things [like] that would just remind me of being in that helpless situation. Even when people say things to me, it isn't right. I went in the next day and made him apologize to me. And there were all these people standing around. I said, "I sprayed you because I felt like I was in a helpless situation." And I apologized to him, because I don't ever want to hurt anybody. And I said, "I want you to apologize to me." He did, in front of all those people. And everybody was looking at me like, wow, she's got a lot of guts. I don't let guys get away with anything now. I feel that men have ruined my life a lot of times. It was hard to get past that.

As I listened to narratives like Angel's, I felt the women's incredible rage at their victimization, while realizing their frustration at having so few social and psychological options at their disposal, resources that would allow them to deal with this anger effectively. In keeping with gender scripts, women are taught to internalize their anger, making it more likely that they will turn rage on themselves rather than direct it externally. Even when they try to violently act out, some, like Angel, are consistently overpowered by their abusers. This creates a kind of pressure-cooker situation for these women—with more degradation and victimization heaped on without intervention, relief, or healing, they are moved closer to a tipping point. For the women in this study, that resulted in violence.

Mo is a homeless woman with a long, turbulent history of victimization and perpetration of violence that began in childhood. As a young teen, she tried to fight back against her father. When she did this, he called the police, and she was charged with domestic violence, again demonstrating the futility of self-protective efforts. Eventually, Mo's school reported her father's abuse. Mo recalls that "they made [my mother] come get me and I lived with her for a couple of years but after so many years of taking all my dad's crap, when I got there, I started beating the shit out of her." Mo also violently attacked her stepmother, stabbing her multiple times. "And we were fighting and I guess after so many years of dealing with so much crap I snapped and took it out on her. So I stabbed her. . . . I stabbed her repeatedly in the head, neck, arm and then I bit a hunk out of her arm. I was really—I had a lot of pent-up anger." The stepmother sustained injuries, and Mo served jail time for this attack. Mo's references to her victimization as years of taking "crap" and having "pent-up anger" again indicate the idea of a tipping point, where violence emerges as a strategy of coping with and resisting cumulative degradations and abuses along the continuum of sexualization. Yet with few other resources at her disposal, Mo's violent solution sends her into a system of incarceration and further social exclusion, which does little to address the underlying context for and sources of her violence.

Once their anger and rage were channeled into violence, the women often continued these behaviors despite physical and emotional costs. Vivi described an abusive relationship in which her boyfriend choked her while she was pregnant. But she "beat up" her ex from another relationship, hitting him with her car, among other behaviors. She admits, "I'm pretty abusive myself. I'm not exactly the nicest person. I can get pretty bad. . . . I have a lot of anger in me, from I don't know where yet. Still working on that." Both Mo and Vivi can identify feelings of anger that precipitate their violence, feelings that are situated in a more nuanced and complex context. Vivi does acknowledge abuse from her father and boyfriends, and although she has gone through anger-management courses, seen a psychiatrist, and taken the prescription drug Zoloft, she feels little peace. What she feels instead is the ever-present rage. Put in a violent situation again, she asserts, "I'd fight him the whole way. I'd never give in." Samantha, who was arrested for beating up her husband, is also unapologetic in the attitude about her violence. She describes a situation where she was violent with her husband when he accused her of infidelity, which she interpreted as an attempt to control her. She says, "And no one owns me. . . . I think that's a double standard. I don't think a man should tell me what to do with my body. He pushed me and I got mad. I don't even think it's a misdemeanor. It's no big deal." It is significant that Samantha specifically references "ownership" of her body, which posits her interpretation of her lived experiences within larger patriarchal contexts. As a dancer and escort, she deals with constant objectification and frequent degradation in exchange for money. Her interaction with her husband is one of the few where she is able to resist this type of exploitation along the continuum of sexualization.

The tipping point into violence for some was triggered by a specific event that facilitated a new mindset. For April, this event was one particular beating by her boyfriend that occurred as he also tried to take their child, to whom April had just given birth. "I put him through a sliding glass door. I picked up a big, heavy office style chair that we had in our apartment and threw it at him and he went through the door. Because he was trying to beat me and take my child from me and I just came home from the hospital with her. So that ain't working." In this case, the boyfriend went to jail, but they got back together when he got out. April asserts that he never beat her again: "No, because he was afraid I was gonna beat him. He found out that I wasn't as scrawny as I looked." The tipping point that compelled Diane to violently resist also related to her children; she blamed her husband for their removal from the home by protective services. She states:

> That's when I actually started lashing back. That's when I decided I'm not taking this anymore and I would fight back. I would always lose, but I would—I actually started being violent with him. When he would swing at me, I'd swing right back. And when he started getting me down on the ground choking me, I'd scratch, I'd bite, I'd kick, I'd do anything I had to do and I never did that before. I just always took it. . . . I did whatever I had to do to get him to understand, look, this isn't happening anymore. I'm not gonna take this anymore, I'm either gonna fight back—
> I'm gonna kill you, you're gonna kill me. Something's gonna happen here. One of us is gonna end up dead. It definitely is survival.

Although Diane continued to be physically overpowered by her husband, her violence began when she realized that she had nothing left to lose—she would fight, or she would die. For her, it was a matter of no longer being able to endure under the existing conditions; it was a refusal to "take it" anymore.

Typically, women who kill their abusers rarely attempt to do so during an attack, and this has been problematic in securing immunity from prosecution for these women, since "belated" violence does not fit with the accepted "imminent danger" standard of self-defense (Murdoch 2000). Tracy, a homeless woman who worked as a prostitute for twenty-seven years, says that she has been in more than sixty situations where she was the victim or perpetrator (or both) of violence. Her relationships were severely violent and after one horrific physical and sexual attack she attempted to kill her abuser.

I tried to kill my last two kids' father. The one that broke the 18 bones on me. One day he beat me so bad he knocked my shoulder off the socket, broke five of my ribs. Busted two of my teeth. Kicking me and everything. And after he done, he said to me, "I want to go make love now, before I take you to the hospital." And I went in there, told him to hurry up and get his shit off, and get off of me. He rolled over, he fell asleep on his back. I went in the kitchen, picked up a stew pot, filled it up with water, let it boil, grabbed my butcher knife, threw the hot water on him and cut him from here [indicates upper chest] to here [indicates abdomen]. They charged me with attempted murder. I got sentenced to ten years; I did five out of ten. Because I couldn't say that he beat me, because every time I had to go to the hospital I had to come up with a story. . . . Because he would stand there and tell me, "If you tell them that I did this, you're gonna get ten times worse than what you got now." You know what I'm saying? So I did it that way. And that's the way life goes.

Avni (1991) points out that the woman who reacts this way may fear for her life and knows she cannot win a physical battle against the stronger abuser. In addition, the woman may feel trapped, since leaving is one of the most dangerous and lethal times for victims of intimate-partner violence (Hardesty 2002). Tracy was also constrained by the threat of more intense beatings if she told the truth about her perpetrator's abuse. Her violence is both self-defense and a response to cumulative victimizations.

Other women interviewed in this study threatened violence or perpetrated violence in adult relationships where there was no abuse at the hands of the current partner, again illustrating the use of violence as a resistance to cumulative victimization along the continuum. Attitudes alone revealed they would consider engaging in violence to preempt further abuse against them in intimate relationships. In Mo's case, she experienced child abuse and was sexually victimized by a number of boyfriends in adulthood. Now, she asserts: "I've been in other relationships, but I tell the guys who I date, I say, if I think you're gonna get physical—the moment I think you're gonna get physical or any type of violence toward me, I'll hurt you first before you can hurt me." Hayley, who had been a victim of intimate-partner violence in three relationships, states: "Because I'm built tough and I'll beat the shit out of a man if he fuckin' ever tries to touch me." These threats materialized in some of the relationships the women described. Ruby says that "men that was violent to me, I didn't do nothing to them. But the one who was sweet to me I'd be violent to." She claims her husband forgives her violence: "He say look, that's alright, because he knows all of my past. I told him most of it. Because of the beatings I been through." Junie makes a statement that is very similar, also indicating her partner's understanding. "He was always telling me you're gonna have to stop slapping me. I don't like that. And I realized—and he understood because of what I went through and he was like, you know, you're just always fighting and that's not the way. And he changed me." Junie and Ruby present evidence rarely brought to light about how the rage and anger experienced by women violently victimized by men can facilitate their resistance to and even violence against supportive and nonviolent male partners.

The vast majority of the women in the case studies here had lives characterized by cumulative violent victimization and marginalization, which had infiltrated and distorted every single aspect, not in one or two situations, but over and over again. Violence truly then became the dominant aspect of existence in almost every way, and rage began to manifest itself physically. Rena exemplifies this—she has one of the longest histories of perpetrating violence, including being charged with the crimes of aggravated assault with a firearm, attempted murder (of an ex-girlfriend), arson, and domestic violence (she broke her partner's arm twice. She has spent time in prison on three different occasions. As discussed earlier, Rena also has one of the longest histories of being a victim of sexual violence, beginning in third grade when she was raped by a school janitor and continuing with rapes and beatings throughout her life. Rena's story leaves no question about her lived experiences of despair and disintegration and the contexts in which these occur.

The contexts from which effects of the continuum of sexualization emerge for the women discussed here—in the formation of their dreams and goals, decisions, further victimization, and perpetration—are closely aligned with Richie's (1996) description of "gender entrapment." Gender entrapment occurs when some women, particularly the most disadvantaged and marginalized (specifically low-income women of color in Richie's study), are, quite literally, set up to fail in the current social arrangements. Despite their deep desire to conform to convention, they are left with "no good, safe way to avoid the problematic social circumstances that they find themselves in, unable to change their social position, and ultimately blamed for both" (Richie 1996, p. 3). The theory of gender entrapment helps explain links between experiences along the continuum of sexualization, starting with gender socialization or "culturally constructed gender-identity development" (Richie 1996, p. 4), violence in intimate relationships, and the dearth of beneficial *survival* options for marginalized women, ultimately resulting, for some, in participation in illegal activities, including violence. According to the Department of Justice, in the general US population the lifetime chances of a woman going to state or federal prison are 1.8 percent (Bonczar 2003). As is typical with most crimes and offenders, only a small proportion of the women who commit crimes are arrested and convicted. Still, among the sample of homeless women we surveyed in the quantitative results for *Hard Lives, Mean Streets* (Jasinski et al. 2010), nearly half of the sample had spent some time in prison or jail at some point in their adult lives, an amount exponentially higher than women in general. Chapter 3 identified some numbers related to the proportion of incarcerated women who experienced childhood sexual abuse. In the quantitative portion of our study (Jasinski et al. 2010), experiences of childhood and adult victimization among the homeless women were strongly and significantly associated with having spent time in jail or prison. Further, homeless women who left their childhood home owing to violence were one and a half times more likely to have spent time in jail or prison. I emphasize that this is a huge injustice and disservice to women in society in the same manner that Ferraro (2006) talks about the population of incarcerated women she studied: "These women's stories substantiate the arguments offered by Chesney-Lind, Bortner and Williams, and Gaarder and Belknap, that the criminal processing system often fails to protect young women and girls from sexual victimization, but holds them accountable when their own behavior results in harm to others" (p. 29). This is entrapment, from all sides.

Accumulating Effects

The cumulative effects of lived experiences along the continuum of sexualization are damaging and severe for the exotic dancers and homeless women in the case studies and serve to illustrate the ways these effects can take shape. Raphael (2004) notes, "If your body does not present limits to other people, you begin to feel that you do not have a right to exist, to take up space" (p. 164). Indeed, repeated violations early on compromised the participants' recognition of and resistance to exploitation as adults, heightening their vulnerability to further harm. It also contributed to many of the psychological effects described in Chapter 4, including depression. Marion describes it as follows:

> You give up. You give up trying. I think the abuse had a lot to do with it. The liquor a lot, too. But the abuse, you keep on having these failed relationships. You think somebody, they're supposed to love you, calm you. And started from your childhood. All these people harm you, your family harm you, your husbands harm you, your boyfriends harm you. You say, you know, there's no use to even trying to do something. 'Cause I get up, somebody going to knock me down.

The interviews told me that, prior to the feelings of hopelessness, as described by Marion, there were clear points at which they had planned on more stable and fulfilling futures. But as the effects of their experiences along the continuum of sexualization emerged, these plans disintegrated and dreams became nightmares. In Chapter 6, I will discuss some ways to change this tragic outcome.

6

How Can We Stop Failing Girls and Women?

I'm always thinking about all that bad stuff. And then I've been through so much trauma in the last couple of years that I just felt so beat down and so lost and I'm asking myself, how did I go from self-sufficient, taking care of myself, to I was losing everything? It all goes back to there's something that's wrong with me. When you hear that for so long, it's hard to get out of the pattern of thinking there's something wrong with you, and then you end up like this, and you're like, well, I guess they were right all along. I am worthless, I am useless, I am unlovable. You know? You just beat yourself up worse. —*Natalie, age 56*

When we ignore the existence and the effects of the continuum of sexualization, we ignore the social problems it creates and perpetuates. We ignore wave after wave of youth who fail to reach their potential or to be productive members of society. We ignore those who grow up to be walking ghosts, scarred in ways that could have been prevented. We ignore girls and women who then turn to the streets, become homeless, or engage in sex work. Chapters 2 and 3 detailed many of the harmful experiences along the continuum of sexualization, and Chapters 4 and 5 explicated the range of possible consequences of the continuum. In this chapter, I engage the continuum of sexualization to identify key areas where we fall short of raising healthy girls in our society. As I recognize various areas of concern, I will examine possible strategies to ameliorate these issues. Changes need to occur at the structural level, with challenges to ideology and social attitudes that perpetuate gender inequality. This top-down approach must be in harmony with a bottom-up effort, where we focus on programs and services that can affect individual lives.

The New Girls' Movement (HGHW 2001) identifies several spheres of influence that are key indicators for effective programming for girls. The first of these is the individual level, which focuses on increasing girls' knowledge, skills, and self-esteem. The second is the social network level, where programs work to create stronger relationships among girls, their families, and their friends. The third level is the community level, which aims to create broader opportunities for girls that challenge unproductive values and belief systems that generate damaging experiences for girls. Finally, the fourth level is institutional, where action focuses on social change activities that impact institutional and systemic practices and norms affecting girls and communities (p. 8). In this chapter, the central areas of concern I pinpoint will be synced with realistic, attainable schemes for improvement that can be implemented for girls and women across these various levels.

Healthy Growth

Earlier, I identified some serious problems in the ways that girls view themselves in terms of both identity and body as they grow into adolescence and then adulthood. All girls experience harmful sexualization. As I have noted, there are certainly structural factors that contextualize both experiences along and effects of the continuum of sexualization, mitigating or exacerbating its destructiveness. Nonetheless, no girl is able to avoid it completely. Inherent in gender socialization, pornified sexualization is part of what girls learn and how their sense of self is shaped as they grow. Therefore, one essential component of any strategy to maximize healthy growth for girls is to address the social construction of gender. Challenges to conventional gender socialization should ideally pervade all aspects of society, from individual identity to larger social attitudes and norms.

> Girls' developmental challenges should always be linked to the larger contexts in which girls grow up. This means more than acknowledging the peer, school, family and community environ-

ments in which girls are embedded, but documenting specifically how gender inequalities and male privilege run through each of these contexts to present challenges to girls at every stage of their lives. (Chesney-Lind & Irwin 2008, p. 124)

One approach is to empower young girls to recognize the artificial nature of gender socialization themselves and provide them with the tools to resist and reshape roles. Programs must offer girls real opportunities to gain status and prestige, rather than placing them into gender-stereotyped categories that reproduce negative messages about girls. "In concrete terms, this would mean offering girls something more than programs that encourage them to be 'nice,' 'kind,' 'well liked,' and 'popular,' but that encourage them to be great thinkers, athletes, scientists, writers" (Chesney-Lind & Irwin 2008, p. 124). This programmatic approach "would acknowledge the larger structural context in which girls grow up, would praise and value girls instead of blaming them for the challenges they confront" (2008, p. 125). Such programs have the potential to impact greater social change, as more girls are made aware that gender identity scripts are not immutable and that there are many more possibilities for them as they grow into young women.

Such an endeavor has been introduced into some recent innovative programming for girls. The Ms. Foundation for Women's Collaborative Fund for Healthy Girls/Healthy Women is a partnership among researchers, funding agencies, girls, women, and staff. In existence since 1996, the Collaborative Fund awards grants to organizations that aim to enhance the strengths of girls ages 9–18 and to young women who staff the organizations. Often these funded programs begin as start-ups with little history upon which to rely in predicting success. Through strategic development based on listening to girls and adolescents talk about their lives and by thoroughly evaluating the limited research, however, effective youth programs for girls have slowly been developed. Data were collected over various phases of design, implementation, and evaluation during the course of three years, and a report, *The New Girls' Movement: Implications for Youth Programs* (HGHW 2001), was produced. In the report, HGHW provides information about twelve of the funded, successful programs across the United States. The report also discloses vital indicators and critical components of effective programs for girls. It is one of the few sources that identify the need not only for gender-specific programming for girls but also for programming that pointedly challenges static perceptions of gender identity.

> To be fully effective for girls and boys, the design and operation of a program must consider gender—not in a manner that regards gender differences as innate and unchangeable, but in a way that explores the social construction of gender and invites young women and men to challenge gender norms, examine gender privilege, and create a balance of power between girls and boys. (HGHW 2001, p. 6)

What is further heartening about the HGHW report is that it acknowledges the fluidity and complexity of identity. In Chapter 2, I emphasized my concern that complicated, developing aspects of female identity were being starved out of existence as the performance of pornified sexualization dominated and consumed the energy, time, and attention of young girls and teenagers. The warning signs are there, but the fact that some services look to foreground the complexity of self provides some assurance. "Our findings demonstrate that youth programs need to support girls as they negotiate these complex intersections and explicitly address the multiple identities each girl carries with her" (HGHW 2001, p. 7). Some of the identity intersections determined in this report include the gendered ways girls experience race, class, and culture.

Challenging concepts of gender identity as unchangeable and embracing the fluidity of identity must be accompanied by strategies that directly address the complicated relationship that girls have with their bodies. "Our research shows that girls are tremendously ambivalent about their bodies, feeling both delight in their physical selves and betrayal as they receive negative messages and attention from the media and society" (HGHW 2001, p. 7). Self-worth is deeply affected by the stereotyped and degraded portrayals of women's pornified sexualization in outlets such as the media, as discussed at length in Chapter 2. There has been a call to address these images through media literacy campaigns for youth: "Because the media are important sources of sexualizing images, the development and implementation of school-based media literacy training programs could be key in combating the influence of sexualization. There is an urgent need to teach critical skills in viewing and consuming media, focusing specifically on the sexualization of women and girls" (APA 2007, p. 4). In fact, the American Psychological

Association released a flier called "Empowering Girls: Media Literacy Resources" as part of their larger report. This provides a list of resources that can be used to help youth become savvy about navigating media messages. It states that with the help of adults, "girls and boys can gain media literacy skills, can learn to resist the message that how girls look is what matters, and can learn how to advocate for themselves" (APA 2007, attachment). What must be included in media literacy education for children and teenagers in order to counter toxic messages about sexuality? Information about "sex stereotyping, damaging effects of the media's sexualization of children, [and] recommendations for ways to discuss these issues with children of different ages" should be included in media literacy (Farley 2009, p. 162). Indeed, long-term goals of the APA initiative are further to "develop age-appropriate multimedia education resources representing ethnically and culturally diverse young people . . . to help facilitate effective conversations about the sexualization of girls and its impact on girls, as well as on boys, women and men" (APA 2007, p. 6).

The reality that youth must be empowered as agents in the construction of their own identities and bodies justifies providing them with the skills to suss through images about media messages themselves. At the same time, early stages of development do not allow for this kind of critical thinking. As noted in Chapter 2, "today's children are bombarded with large doses of graphic sexual content that they cannot process and that are often frightening (Levin 2009, p. 84). Another suggestion for the youngest children, then, is simply limiting exposure to sexual imagery and content (Levin 2009). Of course, this puts the onus on individual parents to monitor exposure to media, which is effective only to the extent that a parent has control over it. Since media images are so omnipresent, another possibility is that when children are exposed to these messages, "expect them to work them out in their play, art and conversations" (Levin 2009, p. 86) and "teach alternative lessons to the messages in popular culture that undermine healthy sexual development and behavior" (p. 87). Age appropriateness is therefore an essential consideration in media literacy education.

Comprehensive, age-appropriate sexual education is also essential for the healthy growth of girls. "Children blog about their need for sex education, and not only regarding the anatomy and physiology of sex. They describe a need for education in how to develop intimate relationships" (Farley 2009, pp. 161–162). Sex education should thus go beyond biology and encompass the more affective components of a burgeoning sexual self, for both boys and girls. This kind of "straight talk" is absent from most dialogue with children and youth about sex. Funded sex education in schools has been focused on abstinence, and this sort of policy is "fueled by politics and polemic" (Tolman 2002, p. 202) rather than science and research about sexual health. This is fundamentally unfair to youth in our society. "To deny adolescents their sexuality and information about it, rather than to educate them about the intricacies and complexities and nuances of their feelings, choices, and behaviors, is to deny them a part of their humanity" (Tolman 2002, p. 203). To put it another way, abstinence-only education does not prevent adolescents from having sex, nor does comprehensive sex education increase the likelihood that they do have sex. Instead, comprehensive sex education increases safe behaviors such as the use of contraception by sexually active teens and provides others with tools to deal with sexual feelings in ways that do not have to include intercourse. I discussed in Chapter 2 how the media have become, by default, the source of sex education for youth. "The outspoken efforts of certain segments of society to preach sexual abstinence until marriage (and without the benefit of meaningful sex education), while at the same time enabling media and corporations to market sex to children more or less as they choose, are untenable and irresponsible" (Levin 2009, p. 87). One repercussion of this for girls is that their sexualization becomes cleaved apart from their sexuality. Without meaningful education about their bodies and accompanying feelings, girls become less actively involved in decisions made about those bodies and increasingly indifferent, passive recipients as actions happen to them. Again, this points to a need for programming that helps girls understand how the expectations for their gender are socially constructed and can be resisted and reconsidered:

> Even to acknowledge the dilemma of desire, we have to be aware both of our strong, embodied and passionate sexual feelings and of the limited and oppressive ways these feelings are discussed or ignored in our own communities and cultures. It is crucial that girls understand that their desire feels like a dilemma as a direct result of social constructions of gendered sexuality. . . . They need to see how our conceptions of male and female sexuality are social constructions that produce privilege and oppression. (Tolman 2002, p. 199)

A responsible society provides planned and funded sex education that not only covers the basics but also frames sexual feelings as a normal part of development and provides teens with realistic ways to process and absorb those feelings that are safe and healthy.

Resilience

Beyond attention to development, what sorts of services can we engage to keep girls healthy and minimize their risks for adverse consequences ranging from emotional problems to delinquency? Resilience is defined as "the psychological ability to successfully cope with severe stress and negative life events" (OJJDP 2009, p. 1). There are a number of directions from which we can approach the concept of resilience in girls and a number of ways we can therefore fortify it. As has been demonstrated, growing up female in a gendered world itself can chip away at resilience, and protective and risk factors coexist in a precarious balance along the continuum of sexualization. Experiences ranging from pornified sexualization to sexual abuse all potentially tip the scales toward risk and diminish resilience. We must also consider resilience in light of the larger structural contexts of poverty, racism, social exclusion, and other marginalizations in which these experiences occur, since contexts further shape protective and risk factors for each individual girl. These many intersections and levels are complicated. Keeping in mind this complexity, I look here at some of the protective factors that shore up resilience and ask: How do we minimize girls' risks along the continuum of sexualization or the fallout from experiences along it?

The US Office of Juvenile Justice and Delinquency Prevention produced a bulletin about resilient girls and factors that protect girls from delinquency (OJJDP 2009) as part of the larger Girls Study Group Series. This study was, in part, motivated by the reality that factors associated with resilience may not be the same for both genders. Another part of the agenda revolved around the need to focus on protective factors rather than risk factors for girls. The bulletin noted that by the time risk factors are identified, it may be too late, since interventions after sexual abuse has occurred, for instance, are not nearly as effective (or essential) as preventing the victimization in the first place. The bulletin published findings from a study that used data from the National Longitudinal Study of Adolescent Health to find out, first of all, if certain protective factors mitigate the potential for girls to engage in destructive behaviors (e.g., delinquency). The four protective factors were the presence of a caring adult, school connectedness, school success, and religiosity. Second, the study sought to determine if these protective factors operated differently when girls were already exposed to known risks for delinquency, particularly personal victimization (e.g., physical and sexual abuse) and structural constraints (e.g., poverty and social exclusion). This combination of individual and contextual components is particularly useful as it transcends just one level and provides a more holistic view of potential risks in a girl's life.

The OJJDP study (2009) found that when risk factor categories were controlled, the extent to which girls believed that an adult cared about them served as a protective factor against delinquency. School success was also significant as a protective factor during adolescence when at-risk girls were not included. When at-risk girls were included in the data, the interaction of protective and risk factors made for more convoluted findings about the nature of resilience. Sadly, it was found that protective factors can be overcome by risk factors and wear down girls' resilience. A risk factor can modify the effects of a protective factor in three ways:

1. By enhancing the protective effect (i.e., the benefits of a protective effect keep a problem behavior from occurring).
2. By attenuating the protective effect (i.e., weakening the beneficial effect).
3. By negating the beneficial effect or by changing the direction of the effect (i.e., the protective effect in the general population is not protective in the at-risk population or is associated with increased negative behavior). (2009, pp. 6–7)

The bulletin provides a table (p. 7) about each risk factor and protective factor and its interaction and effect on the likelihood of delinquent behavior. For example, if a girl was sexually assaulted as a child, school success reduced the likelihood that she would commit simple assault in adolescence. If a girl was physically assaulted as a child, the presence of a caring adult was one factor that decreased the likelihood that she would become involved in property crime in adolescence. The study stopped short of combining together several risk or protective factors, so the outcome is limited in this way. The authors also point out that these findings cannot be generalized to girls who are deeply entrenched in the juvenile justice system. Because the data surveyed a nationally representative sample of teenagers, however, "these data can reveal when factors protect the average adolescent girl from engaging in delinquent behaviors" (OJJDP 2009, p. 8). Overall, the most consistently protective effect in this study was the degree to which an average adolescent girl felt she had caring adults in her life. It is interesting that this factor is corroborated by other research among girls who grow up in more vulnerable and at-risk environments. Those Schaffner (2006) interviewed in juvenile detention, for instance, stated that having a stable relationship with a caring adult was what they needed most to help them cope with the violence they endured in their everyday lives. From the "average" adolescents to those girls in the highest "risk" categories, then, a supportive, involved adult bolsters resilience. This is significant in terms of programmatic considerations, since understanding the role of protective factors can assist in the effective creation of programs to prevent future or additional delinquency among all girls.

Risk, Realized

In general, girls are at risk for a range of destructive experiences along the continuum of sexualization, and certain types of support and programming have the potential to protect from more harm or destructive effects. One significant point that I make throughout this book is while the continuum of sexualization applies to all girls, it applies to all girls differently. So when we ask how to stop failing girls and women, it is important to avoid a monolithic response. Again, context is key. Girls and young women who have multiple, ongoing, severe experiences along the continuum of sexualization and who grow up in contexts of poverty and social exclusion, like the exotic dancers and homeless women I refer to in this book, have fewer skills and resources available to help mitigate their vulnerabilities than a girl growing up in a more advantaged environment. Given the reality for girls, perhaps a better turn of phrase for the most vulnerable is in-risk instead of at-risk, according to Lateefah Simon, executive director at the Center for Young Women's Development in San Francisco (one of the twelve funded HGHW programs and the site for the *Girl Trouble* documentary [Leban & Szajko 2004]). The girls who have lives so fraught with multiple traumas and disadvantages truly are already in-risk.

The urban African American girls interviewed by Miller (2008) are one such in-risk group. They experienced violence systematically and as an overlapping aspect of their neighborhoods, communities, and schools. Though the young women try to "insulate themselves from such violence, they do so in a context in which ideologies about gender work against them at every turn" (p. 192). Girls in such highly disenfranchised and dangerous circumstances have experiences along the continuum of sexualization that permeate their daily lived experiences. As first referred to in Chapter 5, "gender entrapment" (Richie 1996) occurs when multiply marginalized women are, in essence, set up to fail in the current social arrangements. Despite attempts to achieve a "normal" life, they are left with "no good, safe way to avoid the problematic social circumstances that they find themselves in, unable to change their social position, and ultimately blamed for both" (Richie 1996, p. 3). If they run away to escape victimization, Chesney-Lind and Irwin (2008) point out that this population of young women is confronted with terrible choices, "since [they do] not want to return to an intolerable home, yet [they] cannot legally go to school, get employment or find housing without risking return.... Even systems that want to explore other sorts of placement possibilities face numerous challenges, not the least of which is a shortage of programs for girls" (p. 85). The resultant deficit of beneficial survival options for disadvantaged girls and women can lead to living on the streets, engaging in survival sex or prostitution, or participation in other illegal activities.

Some girls and women living on the margins briefly surface in temporary shelters. In Chapter 4, I noted that homeless women in the case study tried to disrupt what they saw as a "cycle of violence" in their lives but had trouble doing so without outside support and intervention (Wesely & Wright 2009). The women were all interviewed at a homeless shelter, which provided some basic services that assisted in their efforts to disrupt the cycle of violence "from the inside out." This was a temporary shelter with limited resources, but it furnished case managers, mental health and addiction treatment, and group therapy sessions. The shelter also had transitional housing on site and provided job and budgeting skills education (including a shelter account where residents deposited money to be used upon their departure). The women's struggles were not as dire once they entered the shelter and were able to resolve immediate fears about safety on the streets as they received these basic services. The women were subsequently less preoccupied with day-to-day survival and more able to work through some of the existing trauma that had so deeply affected them. Junie stated:

> Yeah, [my mom] used to hit me a lot. I just thought that maybe she didn't love me, you know. And I just thought she didn't love me, because she [was] always on me and I was a really good student, and I did everything she wanted at home, so I couldn't understand why she was always hitting me. But then later on I realized that her mother was the same with her. Her mother would hit her and stuff.

Mo, who was physically abused by her father and spent time on the streets, utilized the shelter's parenting classes: "I've caught myself and there was one instance where I didn't catch myself and I did lash out [physically] at [my son] and I felt really crappy for it afterwards. And right now, I'm going to parenting classes [at the shelter] to break the cycle." Diane sees shelter counseling as enabling her to more objectively perceive cycles of violence in her life:

> It started out at nineteen or eighteen. I mean, I ran away from home—I got out and got married and started having kids just to get away from that. And if I wouldn't have been brought up the way I was brought, maybe things would have been different. Maybe I would have went to school. Maybe I would have waited to have kids and my life would have been more stable and things wouldn't have happened the way they happened. I'm not ever gonna regret having my kids but I could have waited. I mean, I didn't have to have two kids at twenty years old. So it's—everything plays into everything. It's a cycle and now that I sit back and look at it, since I've been [at the homeless shelter] I've gotten into counseling.

Already "in-risk," the women's need to avail themselves of comprehensive services was only partially met by the temporary stay at the shelter. At the same time, the most basic programs alone enabled them to gain a modicum of stability. This underscores the missed opportunities early on where so many services could have reached them and prevented further victimization and marginalization, rerouting their lives for the better—if only such programs had existed.

When services and resources for the most in-risk girls and women are so minimal and temporary, however, odds increase that those among this population will not be permanently lifted out of desperate conditions, but instead will move in and out of short-term protection and survival strategies. Since, as I have discussed, survival strategies are often criminalized, quite a few girls end up being ensnared early on in the criminal justice system. Despite the overall drop in juvenile crime, girls are the fastest growing segment of the juvenile justice population, with delinquency cases involving girls increasing by 83 percent between 1988 and 1997 (ABA & NBA 2001). Part of this increase is due to society's changing response to girls' behavior. The "rising arrest rates for girls is partly due to the rampant re-labeling of behaviors that were once categorized as status offenses (non-criminal offenses like 'runaway' and 'person in need of supervision') into violent offenses" (Chesney-Lind & Irwin 2008, p. 174). Once in juvenile detention, there continue to be myriad problems in the treatment of girls that only exacerbate their trauma, anger, and depression and stymie healthy growth. Before delving into suggestions for girls' services once they are in the juvenile justice system, then, I first want to reiterate the nature of *in*effective patterns and approaches that persist.

Gender is the strongest factor in predicting a person's likelihood to break the law, but historically, researchers (who were mostly male) thought it unnecessary to include women or girls in their samples (Belknap 2007). "That is, rather than include in the study a means of assessing how girls' lives might be different from boys' lives, girls' delinquency has typically been viewed as peripheral and unnecessary to understanding juvenile offending and processing" (Belknap 2007, p. 4). The "pathways" approach, most common to feminist criminology, recognizes the life histories of girls and women and engages them to clarify relationships between childhood and adult traumas and criminal offending by girls and women. Consistent with the pathways model, we know that the experiences along the continuum of sexualization, particularly severe, frequent ones in terms of sexual abuse and exploitation at young ages, play a significant role in the lives of at-risk young girls, can lead to gender entrapment and criminalized victimization, and may route them into the juvenile justice system. As discussed in Chapter 3, girls are disproportionately charged with status offenses such as running away. Though running away is an escape or survival strategy, a girl arrested for this offense is punished rather than protected. The fact that girls are disproportionately charged with status offenses has been attributed to a variety of factors, including

> bias in discretionary decisions by police, probation, prosecutors, judges and agency personnel to handle runaway and other status offending girls through the delinquency system. The legal mechanisms that contribute to this disparate processing include violations of valid court orders, contempt proceedings, probation and parole revocations, misdemeanor charges associated with running away, and charges of escape, absconding and AWOL (Absent Without Official Leave). (ABA & NBA 2001, p. 17)

In addition to the arrest, charging, and filing stemming from the overattention to girls' status offenses, a gender bias against girls has also been found in terms of detention. Not only has the detention rate increased for girls, but also there is ample evidence that they are being detained for offenses that are less serious than those of boys. Often these include violations of probation or parole. In the documentary *Girl Trouble* (Leban & Szajko 2004), it was noted that the lack of programs for girls while in the juvenile justice system (an issue that will be examined in greater detail below) increased the likelihood that they would be given "conditions of probation" instead of being assigned to participate in established programs, which already exist for boys. Conditions of probation might include adhering to curfew, attending school, or being sporadically drug tested. These structured restrictions mean that if a girl fails and is caught violating the conditions, she can be returned to the system. All the while, none of the underlying causes of her original or continued offending are addressed, and she becomes more and more deeply immersed in the criminal justice process.

According to a study of several US cities conducted by the Annie E. Casey Foundation's Juvenile Detention Alternative Initiative (JDAI), "many more girls than boys are detained for minor offenses such as public disorder, probation violations, status offenses and traffic offenses . . . the JDAI study also found that girls are more likely than boys to be detained for probation and parole violations (54% girls versus 19% boys in another study site)" (ABA & NBA 2001, pp. 18–19). Detaining girls in this way once again punishes them instead of treating them. It also reproduces the gender constructs that support the surveillance of girls' bodies, with "detention as a means of social control" (ABA & NBA 2001, p. 19). The formalizing of social control over girls via the juvenile justice system pushes increasing numbers of girls into the system "for offenses that were previously either ignored or labeled as non-violent offenses" (Chesney-Lind & Irwin 2008, p. 183). The ABA and NBA (2001) additionally report that girls are more likely than boys to be returned to detention after release, even though their rates of recidivism are lower than that of boys. In part, this may be owing to the fact that girls tend to more often be cited for contempt, and contempt offenders are more frequently detained than noncontempt offenders. Even without committing a new crime, then, girls are more likely than boys to be sent back to detention. Of the four JDAI US cities from which data were collected, girls comprised only 14 percent of the total detention population but made up 30 percent of those returned to detention within one year. Chesney-Lind and Irwin (2008) remark that one of the most alarming aspects of their findings is that "increased policing of girls' relatively minor behavior has resulted in dramatic increases in their arrest, detention, referral to court, and most recently, their incarcerations" (p. 183). Serious repercussions for the consistent increase in girls detained and incarcerated in juvenile system facilities include major overcrowding (several juvenile placements for girls had mattresses on the floor and used common rooms as sleeping areas), poor conditions of confinement, and the reduction of appropriate services for girls (ABA & NBA 2001).

Much to the detriment of female offenders, the juvenile justice system overall has not attended to gender differences in a positive way at any of the stages that bring girls into or process them through the system.

> The juvenile justice system's reaction to these differences has not been the development of gender-responsive policy and programming. The current system has been designed to deal with the problem of boys and young men and, in doing so, has neglected the gender-specific programming and treatment needs of girls and young women. Girls and young women respond differently than young males to program interventions and treatment. These differences in system response and individual reaction to treatment require separate research and planning to meet the needs of young females enmeshed in a system designed to manage and serve a predominantly male population. (Bloom & Covington 2001, p. 3)

Indeed, "there is a glaring dearth of appropriate, developmentally sound, culturally competent, gender-specific prevention, diversion and treatment programs for girls in the justice system" (ABA & NBA 2001, p. 4), and the rise in detention rates is but one of many reasons. The reality is that only about 4 percent of federal health and human services funding goes to services for girls (Leban & Szajko 2004; United Way of the Bay Area and the San Francisco Juvenile Probation Department 2003). In one study of 443 delinquency prevention programs, it was found that only 2 percent served only girls and 6 percent served primarily girls (Lipsey 1990). Similar distributions exist in private funding. A 2003 study by the Washington Women's Foundation that reviewed 12,000 grants from District of Columbia–area foundations found that only 7 percent of $441 million dollars went to programs for girls or women (Chesney-Lind & Irwin 2008).

For the highly limited programs that do exist, "most are modeled after programs that serve males. Consequently, girls, and especially minority girls, increasingly are being placed in programs that fail to meet their unique development, physiological and emotional needs" (ABA & NBA 2001, p. 22). I discussed earlier the growing rates of girls of color overrepresented in the system. This is reflected in comparative rates for arrest, detention, sentencing, and long-term incarceration (Schaffner 2006). Such disproportionate minority representation intersects with the overall increase of girls in the system and further directs our attention to where we fall short in attending to these in-risk populations. "Now is the time to replace one-size-fits-all prevention programming with comprehensive approaches tailored to the needs and circumstances of young girls and women" (CASA 2003, p. 75). When the 1974 Juvenile Justice and Delinquency Prevention Act (JJDPA) was reauthorized in 1992, it called for plan development and fairness. "However, parity and fairness do not mean copying males' programs and providing them to females. To be effective, such programs need to meet the specific needs of girls" (Bloom & Covington 2001, p. 6). The JJDPA was most recently reauthorized in 2002, at which point it called for "a plan for providing needed gender-specific services for the prevention and treatment of juvenile delinquency" with funding "for programs that focus on the needs of young girls at risk of delinquency" (Christy Sharp and Jessica Simon [2004], in *Girls in the Juvenile Justice System: The Need for More Gender Responsive Services*, as cited in Chesney-Lind & Irwin 2008).

Now that some of the existing problems in the juvenile justice system have been laid out, we can move on to the question: What *are* these critical unmet needs in programming for delinquent girls ensnared in the juvenile justice system? Paramount and consistent throughout the literature on programs for juvenile girls is the call for attention to the effects of childhood trauma and abuse, especially in the form of sexual victimization. One sample of incarcerated youth revealed that the trauma experienced by girls tended to be victimization by violence, whereas that reported by boys was witnessing a violent event. These delinquent girls also reported significantly higher levels of physical punishment, sexual abuse, and psychological distress than did the delinquent boys (Steiner, Garcia, & Mathews 1997). As detailed in Chapters 3 and 4, the effects of such trauma on girls are numerous and include depression, anxiety, PTSD, sexual adjustment disorders, and behavior dysfunctions such as eating disorders, substance abuse, self-mutilation, and suicide. National studies indicate that both depression and PTSD are high among the population of girls in the justice system (Girls' Justice Initiative 2003). "Studies have consistently found that among those who are exposed to trauma, females are more likely than males to develop mental health problems as a result. . . . If the trauma is not resolved, negative residual effects may result, including (a) alcohol and drug use, (b) involvement in violent activity, and (c) development of mental health problems such as PTSD" (National Child Traumatic Stress Network 2004, p. 4). Without a doubt, the impact of trauma and potential PTSD must be included when evaluating and providing services to delinquent girls in the system (Reebye et al. 2000).

The attendant problem, however, is that since "the courts often lack the necessary training and resources to address or recognize the impact of traumatic experiences, they often lack the capacity to adequately meet the mental health needs of girls who may then end up going deeper into the system" (National Child Traumatic Stress Network 2004, p. 5). Appropriate interventions must affect the juvenile system in three areas to be successful: laws and policies, training of court personnel and staff, and delivery of appropriate projects and programming (Schaffner 2006). When only outwardly displayed behaviors are responded to by any aspect of the system, it is the symptom rather than the source that is being treated. It is not surprising that this fails to solve the behavioral problems for good. "For many of these adolescent females there appears to be a link between the experience of abuse and neglect, the lack of appropriate treatment, and the behaviors that led to arrest" (National Child Traumatic Stress Network 2004, p. 4). For example, existing services have focused on the behavior of running away rather than its root causes. "With the high incidence of girls' runaway behavior, many programs have been focused on control rather than the provision of effective support for girls to become successful and to grow beyond the trauma that often drives their runaway behavior" (ABA & NBA 2001, p. 12). Attempting to control girls' behavior without attention to underlying trauma may exacerbate the negative psychological effects instead of being productive.

> Depression is common but often not diagnosed in delinquent girls; their behavioral problems are typically the focus of intervention rather than their underlying sadness, isolation, sense of loss and early trauma. Girls may react especially negatively to outside controls and be labeled "oppositional," although their aggression is often a self-defense mechanism against past abuse. (ABA & NBA 2001, p. 10)

Tools to heal from trauma must be directly incorporated into all aspects of programming, or girls are unlikely to change the delinquent behaviors that have helped them survive or cope thus far in their lives.

One schema for trauma treatment focuses on three stages of recovery: safety, remembrance and mourning, and reconnection (Herman 1997). Safe space is a "bottom line issue" and perhaps the most critical element of positive girls' programming (HGHW 2001). Safe space describes "a certain set of personal and programmatic relationships, activities and interactions" (HGHW 2001, p. 13) and includes not only safety from violence and comfort in self-expression, but also ways to allow girls to resolve conflicts productively and to develop positive, affirming relationships with other girls and adult women. "It is from this place of security that girls begin to re-envision themselves and engage their families, institutions, and communities in new and transforming ways" (HGHW 2001, p. 13). Safe space also facilitates the second and third stages of recovery in the trauma model, since the more secure girls feel about addressing victimization and loss, the more able they are to do so. Per the third stage, relationships with others are particularly important for girls, and safe space (expounded upon in more detail in the HGHW [2001] report) creates a paradigm for how to foster and maintain these healthy connections.

Schaffner (2006) includes a chapter in her book about girls in trouble with the law that parses the many nuances of what has been known as gender-appropriate, gender-specific, and gender-responsive programming. Even though existing research has recognized the need to move beyond gender-neutral programming for detained girls, the finer details of programming related to gender are far from solid. Schaffner's work is an excellent resource. She notes that one critique of gender-specific policy and programming in the juvenile system has been its potential to perpetuate antiquated notions reinforcing traditional, heterosexual, stereotypic expectations for femininity. To be truly gender appropriate and responsive, programming not only must identify the ways in which gender shapes the pathways to delinquency for girls and address them therapeutically (not just punitively) but also must avoid sexist or homophobic assertions of gender identity or being female. She notes that there is increasing urgency to respond to the growing community of gay, lesbian, bisexual, transgender, queer, and questioning (GLBTQ) youth in juvenile systems. This brings into sharper relief the above imperative for safe spaces for girls in programming.

There are several other crucial unmet programmatic needs for delinquent girls in the juvenile justice system. One of these relates to addressing the survival strategy of prostitution. As I have noted, prostitution is one of the two offenses for which juvenile girls are arrested more than boys and at a disproportionate rate compared to their overall population in the juvenile system. The documentary *Very Young Girls* (Schisgall & Alvarez 2007) chronicles the lives of girls barely into their adolescence who were prostituted and exploited on the streets of New York. The film notes that in the United States the average age of entrée into prostitution is 13 years, which is reflected in the life histories revealed in the film. As one girl states, "At the age of 13, what choices [for survival on the streets] do I have?" It is pointed out that at any other time, a 14-year-old girl is considered by the law too young to consent to sex. But as prostitutes, these girls are criminalized, taken to jail instead of to the hospital. The men that find, exploit, and abuse them are typically more than twice their age, as in the case of Shaneiqua, who was 12 when she was taken in and pimped out by a 30-year-old man. This supports a possible relationship to victimization, since "abuse can reduce a girl's capacity to recognize and protect her physical boundaries, especially when combined with the power differential inherent in sexual relationships between teenage girls and adult males" (United Way of the Bay Area and the San Francisco Juvenile Probation Department 2003, p. 9). Indeed, in Chapter 4, I noted that qualitative research with female prostitutes (Chesney-Lind & Rodriguez 1983; Gilfus 1992; Silbert & Pines 1982) finds that more than half report histories of sexual abuse, many report running away as their first criminal act, and at least one-fourth identify sexual abuse as their reason for becoming prostitutes. Certainly, then, programs that address trauma would be a necessary part of recovery for girls in the juvenile justice system owing to prostitution. Beyond this, however, services are needed for girls to help them permanently break with this lifestyle and find alternatives for sustained livelihood.

The Girls' Justice Initiative, which promotes justice and gender-responsive programming for system-involved girls, conducted interviews with incarcerated girls in five jurisdictions. The executive summary report stated: "The girls we spoke with were particularly concerned that prostitution be addressed in community-based programs and through the services they receive in placement. Consistent with national data, these girls identified prostitution as a source of danger and trauma in their lives" (Girls' Justice Initiative 2003). Programs that focus on prostitution are few and far between. Girls Educational and Mentoring Services (GEMS) is one such program and is the site for the *Very Young Girls* (Schisgall & Alvarez 2007) documentary. The GEMS mission is to empower young women, ages 12–21, who have experienced commercial sexual exploitation and domestic trafficking, to exit the commercial sex industry and develop to their full potential. GEMS provides an alternative to incarceration for about 200 girls a year, typically referred by the courts after a prostitution arrest. Yet it is the only such program in New York State, and similar resources in other states are equally as scarce; a surprising situation when prostitution charges are among the more common for delinquent girls. The director of the Girls' Services Unit at San Francisco's female detention center noted that many of the girls in her unit are there due to prostitution or drug-related charges. "Despite significant numbers of detained girls involved in prostitution, staff at the San Francisco facility noted that they lack the gender and culturally responsive programming needed to address patterns of sexual exploitation and victimization common among detained girls" (Girls' Justice Initiative 2003, p. 8).

Other programmatic needs for incarcerated juvenile girls relate to sex education and pregnancy. In a San Francisco study, approximately one-third of the girls in the juvenile justice system were pregnant or parenting (United Way of the Bay Area and the San Francisco Juvenile Probation Department 2003). This has been seen as a serious issue by those who work in the system. Surveys of juvenile defense attorneys affiliated with the American Bar Association National Juvenile Defender Center and of judges identified by juvenile defense attorneys revealed that when asked to identify specific gaps in girls' programming, the surveyed attorneys and judges named education about sex, sexuality, pregnancy, and parenting. Specifically, 73 percent of attorneys and 51 percent of judges said that their jurisdictions did not have enough programming related to girls with babies, 70 percent of attorneys and 44 percent of judges said their jurisdictions did not have enough programming related to sexual victimization, and 65 percent of attorneys and 35 percent of judges said their jurisdictions did not have enough programs about parenting. The girls across five jurisdictions similarly agreed (Girls' Justice Initiative 2003).

There are other areas identified in the research, by practitioners and by juvenile girls themselves, when it comes to programmatic needs in detention. It is beyond the scope of this book to discuss every single one in detail. Most relevant and striking about many of these findings is that they largely correspond on some level with girls' severely traumatic experiences along the continuum of sexualization and that in fact these early experiences are what tend to shape and propel delinquent behavior for girls (through survival or coping techniques or some combination thereof). For instance, as discussed in Chapter 4, rates of substance abuse are related to those of sexual victimization. "Substance use is one type of coping strategy that can provide escape from painful childhood experiences and serve as a means of self-medication to reduce feelings of isolation and loneliness" (CASA 2003, p. 51). According to CASA, women who were sexually abused as children are more than three times as likely to have symptoms of alcohol dependence and more than 2.5 times as likely to abuse drugs than those who had not been sexually abused (2003). When considering crime, also recall from previous chapters that adult women are overwhelmingly incarcerated for nonviolent offenses, including the violation of laws that prohibit the sale and possession of specific drugs. Female victims of sexual abuse have the highest rates of drug and alcohol related crimes (Chesney-Lind 1997;

Daly 1994; Gilfus 1992). When it comes to juveniles, in one study the rates of self-reported cocaine use among detainees were more than twice as high for girls as for boys (OJJDP 2004). Ten percent of youths detained in the juvenile justice system who reported using drugs said they first used them at or before age 11, and 25 percent reported first use at or before age 12. Ten percent of the juveniles who reported using cocaine said they first used it before age 11, and 50 percent reported first use before age 15 (OJJDP 2004). Substance abuse is gendered, and so, in order to be successful, its treatment must be also. There are intricate overlaps with age, gender, experiences along the continuum of sexualization, and juvenile crime, and these overlaps ought to be addressed in gender-responsive programming for delinquent girls.

If we were to create an ideal template for gender-directed programs for girls in juvenile detention (already in-risk), what would it look like? First, it would devote attention to the pathways that lead girls into criminal behavior at a young age so that early trauma is identified. The gendered ways in which victimization is criminalized for girls, and gender entrapment occurs, accordingly, must guide an understanding of the delinquent acts committed. The most common crimes for delinquent girls are intimately related to experiences along the continuum of sexualization and resulting trauma, deeply embedded survival mechanisms, and coping strategies. Programs fundamentally must provide a safe place to process this sort of chaotic past and allow girls to grieve and heal. Second, the ideal template would integrate services. A few prevention programs have successfully brought together some of these aspects. One of these, called Project Chrysalis, is a school-based, voluntary, substance abuse prevention program targeted at girls in grades nine through twelve who have histories of physical, sexual, and emotional abuse (CASA 2003). The integration of childhood histories of abuse and substance use can also be useful when applied to in-risk populations such as delinquent girls. Cross-integration must also occur at the systemic level, with collaboration between state and county systems and community-based programs. "Access to those gender-specific services requires greater cross-system integration than is currently the rule, development of collaborative approaches between levels and branches of government . . . as well as development of advocacy practices for programs and attorneys representing girls in the system" (ABA & NBA 2001, p. 24). Third, "get-tough" approaches are ineffective for girls and may do more harm than good (this relates to the critical need for girls to feel safe).

> Many characteristics of the detention environment (seclusion, staff insensitivity, loss of privacy) can exacerbate negative feelings and feelings of loss of control among girls, resulting in suicide attempts or self-mutilation. The traditional methods of preserving order and asserting authority in these centers (especially "tough" physically confrontational approaches and the use of isolation or restraints) may backfire with female detainees who suffer from PTSD. (National Child Traumatic Stress Network 2004, p. 5)

This finding is reiterated by CASA (2003) in its discussion of young women's unique needs in substance abuse treatment. Since girls are more likely than boys to have been victimized by physical and sexual abuse, "treatment programs that employ confrontational approaches may be less appropriate for female survivors of such abuse" (p. 9). However well intentioned the creation of such programs, those designed with "tough-on-crime" and "zero-tolerance" initiatives toward youth violence have caught girls up in a trend that does more harm than good (Chesney-Lind & Irwin 2008). Fourth, the ideal programming for delinquent girls should build on strengths rather than deficits. "Focusing on what girls have done wrong alienates them and makes them defensive. . . . Girls feel more capable when their strengths are appreciated, which empowers them to change" (Girls' Justice Initiative 2003, p. 10).

The End Result

Achieving an ideal might be a lofty goal, but it is possible to at least move in the right direction. The reasons for doing so are compelling. Perhaps even more compelling is what happens if we do not improve the situation for girls already in risk. If changes are not made, at minimum we continue the status quo. Right now, the status quo reflects a consistently rising number of girls in juvenile detention, a scenario that, without comparable increases in programs or even in juvenile facilities themselves, results in problems, such as overcrowding, that are discussed above. Between 2001 and 2003, there was a 98 percent rise in the detention of girls (compared to 29 percent for boys) and a 92 percent rise in girls' referrals to juvenile courts (compared to 29 percent for boys) (Chesney-Lind & Irwin 2008). This is extremely detrimental, not just for girls but for society as a whole. Consider that for girls to end up in juvenile detention, they have already been failed at multiple levels. Typically, no prevention, little to no support or intervention, and few resources were available to them as they made their way through painful and often abusive childhoods rooted in contexts of economic marginality and social exclusion. As they grew into their teens, their risks were multiplied by running away, getting involved with negative influences or troubled peer groups, trying to survive on the streets, or committing petty or status offenses. They have already had severe experiences along the continuum of sexualization and by the age of 11 may have used drugs or by the age of 13 may have prostituted or engaged in survival sex. By the time they enter the juvenile justice system, there were many points at which their lives could have been rerouted toward healthier development, but they were not. Now, the girls are in the system.

Let us look at some of the facts about juvenile detention. For one, it is expensive. In San Francisco, the cost of incarcerating a girl is approximately $120/day, depending on her needs. "Use of detention is an expensive option that offers little chance of addressing the needs of girls and changing life outcomes. . . . Money invested in prevention and intervention programs that address the specific needs of girls would save detention dollars, be more cost effective and yield more positive outcomes for girls" (United Way of the Bay Area and the San Francisco Juvenile Probation Department 2003, p. 14). The juvenile justice system typically operates separately from community organizations, a situation that does nothing to preserve girls' connections with familiar neighborhoods, family, and friends. Yet "community-based interventions for system involved girls [*sic*] are a cost-effective, promising alternative to detention, residential programs, and incarceration" (Girls' Justice Initiative 2003, p. 10). Prevention and intervention programs, especially those that are community based, thus have the potential to save money by reducing future detention and incorporate key elements to directly address the problems for in-risk girls.

The population of incarcerated adult women offenders additionally tells us about the juvenile justice system. About 20 percent of adult female offenders also served a sentence as a juvenile. Girls who have been detained in the juvenile system are at high risk for later criminal justice involvement (United Way of the Bay Area and the

San Francisco Juvenile Probation Department 2003). "When the profile of girl offenders is compared to the profiles of adult women offenders, both in prison and in community corrections, it becomes clear that they are essentially the same females moving along the system from juvenile detention to jail or community corrections to state prison" (Bloom & Covington 2001, p. 6). Girls in the system tend to become women in the system, but programs that address root causes of juvenile offenses again have the potential to redirect this path. Substance abuse is an example. I noted earlier that substance abuse is related to other experiences along the continuum of sexualization. "Substance abuse studies indicate that trauma, particularly in the form of physical or sexual abuse, is closely associated with substance abuse disorders in women" (NIJ 2003, p. 80). Yet recent drug policy, which espouses harsh sanctions without services or treatment, perpetuates the rise of women in the criminal justice system.

> Inadvertently, the war on drugs became a war on women, particularly poor women and women of color. . . . The emphasis on punishment rather than treatment has brought many low-income women and women of color into the criminal justice system. Women offenders who in past decades would have been given community sanctions are now being sentenced to prison. Mandatory minimum sentencing for drug offenses has significantly increased the numbers of women in state and federal prisons. (NIJ 2003, p. 62)

In addition, these gender-neutral sentencing laws do not distinguish between major players in drug organizations and minor, peripheral ones (who are typically women). Women are further penalized when they have been convicted of a state or federal drug offense, as they face the lifetime ban on cash assistance and food stamps stipulated in the 1996 Welfare Reform Act. These benefits are essential for women to get back on their feet after incarceration for drugs, not only for sustenance but also for their ability to enter and remain in drug treatment, which research finds is essential to recovery (NIJ 2003). This finding is relevant to a discussion about programs for girls because of the ways that substance use might have been interrupted and treated earlier on. It also speaks to the need to address the earliest trauma that put girls at risk for later substance use.

Girls and young women who have multiple, ongoing, severe experiences along the continuum of sexualization and who grow up in contexts of poverty and social exclusion are at heightened risk and have even fewer skills and resources available to help mitigate their vulnerabilities. The best case scenario is a tandem top-down and bottom-up approach, in which social inequalities that put girls at risk along the continuum of sexualization are addressed along with programs that can foster individual change. In an ideal world, all girls should receive services such as those discussed at the start of this chapter, services that provide education about the development of healthy identity, the skills to be agents of their bodies, and the messages they get about those bodies. The reality is that these preventative measures are not in place for girls, at least not holistically. So, as girls (particularly those who already experience multiple marginalizations) grow into adolescence, they become more at risk. Still, possibilities are there for intervention, if not prevention. When these girls then fall through the cracks, the likelihood increases that they end up in the juvenile justice system. From there, possibilities for positive change are further narrowed as the girls grow up. "For women who are in the system, a gender-responsive approach would include comprehensive services that take into account the content and context of women's lives. Programs need to take into consideration the larger social issues of poverty, abuse, and race and gender inequalities as well as individual factors that affect women in the criminal justice system" (NIJ 2003, p. 88). For those at-risk simply by being girls and for those in-risk and coping with multiple disadvantages, we need to direct attention and resources to their growth.

7
A Challenge to Our Society

The feeling of being homeless is feeling unwanted, feeling not belonging, feeling different. Feeling that people—you're not part of society. That you're separate. You live on a totally different planet. Being abused is almost the same feeling. The abusive want to hurt you. They want to control you. They look at you as a nobody. To me the same feeling is of not belonging, not being loved, being different, living in your own little world. To me, it's the same because both of them are abusive. —*Tamara, age 50*

In this book I contend that the continuum of sexualization is the conceptual core around which any comprehensive discussion of the lived experiences of girls and women must revolve. This was my realization after years of research with populations of girls and women. Findings from my in-depth interviews with these populations revealed the emergence of a relatively consistent range of encounters and events. Though these varied in frequency and form, they were clearly connected through a common theme. Sexualization is this shared thread, and framing it as a continuum appropriately underscores the relatedness between these experiences. I am confident that no analysis of the lived experiences of any individual or population of girls and women is complete without attention to the continuum of sexualization. Each chapter in this book has provided a different dimension of support for this contention.

The argument began with a discussion of gender socialization. Falling on one end of the continuum, the gender socialization of girls is what teaches them that their sexualized embodiment is a major part of their identity and value, even as it is trivialized and degraded. This construction of girls is not an accident; instead, gender socialization is a mechanism through which we not only incorporate meanings of the self but also reproduce dominant power inequalities. The effectiveness of socialization is a testament to how uncritically—indeed, unthinkingly—gender meanings are adopted and internalized. As such, they appear natural and normal, rather than something contrived, constructed, and performed. The inequalities that shape these gender meanings are correspondingly camouflaged.

Girls work hard to attain the look, behavior, demeanor, attitude, and comportment that their gender socialization dictates. They can never work hard enough, however. At earlier and earlier ages, now the "tween" years, girls are directed onto the treadmill of appearance obsession, only to go nowhere, for this fixation with a sexy look grants no real power to the girls. The treadmill moves faster; they expend more energy, time, and resources toward achieving this image at the expense of other areas of development. Indeed, because of the cultural emphasis on their sexualization, girls learn early on to self-objectify and monitor their appearance relentlessly, which distracts them from other pursuits. Yet there is never a feeling of finally attaining the look, only forever working toward it, so the brass ring remains just out of reach. And there is always someone who appears to carry sexiness more successfully, who gets more attention from boys, whose tight T-shirt and low-riding skinny jeans fit more perfectly. If she is not the girl at the nearby lunch table, she is on MTV, on billboards, on Facebook, on reality shows, in movies, in video games. She is even on the Disney channel, where girls who appear just into their teenage years are rail thin but fully developed with perfect hair and skin and sexy, revealing high-fashion clothing. Girls can't avoid seeing this image, and even if they close their eyes, it likely dances behind their lids in the form of the Disney-fied fairy princess who might be able to grant that one wish.

Though gender socialization has always occurred, been directly connected to inequalities, and provided a roadmap for "acceptable" identity for boys and girls, its price on the soul is being ratcheted up exponentially. Raw caricatures of exaggerated female sexiness have pervaded the mainstream. We live in an increasingly pornographic landscape in which our minds, numbed by constant bombardment, only pay attention when images are over the top. This is pornified sexualization, and it is far reaching. The ubiquity of media facilitates the spread of the pornified image, and more and more children and young teens regularly absorb it, thanks to highly accessible technological gadgets. Tweens have become a relentlessly targeted consumer demographic. At these pre-pubescent ages, girls previously remained unconcerned about the opposite sex or appearing sexy, but they are now being marketed (and they—or their parents—are buying) "Porn Star" T-shirts and thong underwear. Fewer alternative images are available for girls as they get pressed from all sides into the pornified sexualization mold, cookie-cutter style. Even though this image is artificial, created through performance and disciplines of the body, it has flooded the culture. In a highly consumptive society where images are bought and sold, girls' bodies have become just another commodity.

In this book I have discussed how, despite the grip of these gender expectations, girls still struggle with identity meanings. They hunger for some real information about their bodies and their sexuality. Yet comprehensive sex education is scarce across the country. In the past several decades, most federally funded sexual education programs have focused on abstinence and provided girls with little actual information about their sexuality or sexual desire. With its overabundance of sexual imagery and messages, media become the de facto source of knowledge about sex. Such skewed material without any other accessible, useful information that might serve as counterbalance increasingly disconnects girls from their own bodies. They may appear to seamlessly adopt and perform the pornified sexual image, but this does little to enrich a solid sense of self, sexually or otherwise. I am reminded of my interviews with the exotic dancers, who both temporarily and permanently altered their bodies in order to perform a pornified image in exchange for money. The more they transformed their physical selves in service to the hyper-sexualized image, the less vital or meaningful their bodies became to their identities. This was revealed in Skye's comment about her breast implants: "And since I got my boobs done, they seem like just part of my costume." Her breasts have now become part of her performance, rather than a part of *her*. Because the body plays a role in creating meanings of selfhood, artificially cleaving it apart from identity is psychologically damaging. "Most people do not think of their bodies as biological things that consist of matter like any other things they encounter from day to day. They equate their bodies with elaborate concepts of selfhood and endow them with very special (superior to other objects) properties" (Fisher 1973, p. 8). The disconnect occurs when the pornified performance substitutes for substance, which is something that can only be nurtured and developed from the inside out.

The continuum of sexualization is clearly unavoidable for girls and women in contemporary Western society when at a minimum they experience the pornified sexualization inherent in gender socialization. This sexualization is its own victimization of women and girls, with the culture as perpetrator. On the other end of the continuum is sexual violence and abuse. With gender socialization on one end and sexual victimization on the other and every conceivable remaining aspect of sexualization in between, the continuum fully encompasses the possible range of experiences girls and women may have in their lifetime, simply by virtue of being female. Though all girls run the gauntlet of gender socialization, this book has also noted that a startlingly high number endure sexual attack, rape, and other forms of invasive physical victimization. What such frequency reveals is that the experiences along the continuum of sexualization are not few and far between for women but are common, sometimes everyday parts of their lives; the continuum is thus woven into the treacherous terrain that girls navigate daily and very early on.

I have shown that these experiences along the continuum of sexualization are not, in any way, beneficial to girls in society. Yet with gender socialization as one of the building blocks of identity, along with a culture in which attitudes and ideology can contribute to sexual violence against girls and women, it is practically from the time of birth that girls must contend with the effects of the continuum of sexualization. Though I have detailed many mental and psychological effects of these experiences, I find the disconnect mentioned above to be one of the most disturbing of all, perhaps because of the ways that this has the potential to seriously compromise the safety and health of girls. First, at the developmental level, it is problematic for girls to devote themselves to success at looking sexy without being educated about what sexuality, sexual identity, or sexual desire means for them. Without this parallel education about their bodies or about how to sift through media critically, the performance of the pornified image eclipses anything real about female sexual growth. This thwarts healthy identity development for girls and creates cognitive dissonance as they try to make sense of contrary messages. It is also socially irresponsible. Both boys and girls need and deserve frank information about their bodies and sexuality. Second, the disconnect corresponds to an increased inability to make informed decisions about the body. Girls who *act* rather than *feel* sexual, or who are unable to separate attention to their appearance from true affection, are growing up with "confused bodies" (Tolman 2002); the actual skills needed in coping with intimacy and sexual feelings are low priority in a culture obsessed with sex(iness). In this environment, a girl's sexual self is only recognized when it is being surveilled, controlled, or exploited.

Third, the fact that girls are disconnected from their bodies potentially makes them feel as though embodied experiences happen to them rather than possessing a feeling of agency in decision-making about their bodies. To feel agency is to have "a sense of autonomy over one's body and desires" (Orenstein 1994, p. 56) and is essential to a healthy and whole adult identity. The estrangement from their bodies coupled with the preoccupation with its external appearance alienates girls from themselves. This has also been referred to as "depersonalization," which occurs when the body does not feel like one's own (Fisher 1973). When a feeling of agency over the body is missing, it is one of the most dangerous aspects of the disconnect engendered by the social construction of girls. Girls still may be sexually active—often starting off in early adolescence—but this is accompanied by riskier behaviors that result from disengagement or passivity concerning their physical selves. One result is the high rates of teen pregnancy and sexually transmitted diseases (STDs) for which teen girls bear a disproportionate burden. In sexual situations, girls can become silenced, unable to give voice to their needs or personal limits owing to the disconnect from their bodies and the absence of a clear sexual identity. Through gender constructions, then, we have actually created a new category of vulnerability to sexual victimization for girls. Girls who are disengaged from their bodies and lack feelings of agency or control over them are less able to create boundaries or assert limits and may be more easily taken advantage of, exploited, and victimized.

When considering the high levels of sexual violence against and abuse of girls and women documented in society, I have pointed out that social ideologies and attitudes that support the pornified sexualization of girls and women play a major role. It is clear that there are many mechanisms through which this occurs. A culture shrouded in these views and expectations of women can only contribute to more detrimental experiences along the continuum of sexualization. This intracontinuum effect has to do, in part, with how pornified sexualized appearance and performance are read as a message of sexual availability or readiness. Assumptions of sexual invitation are not limited to adult women but are also ascribed to children. As the line between girl and adult woman is blurred in sexualized images presented in the mainstream, young girls are made to appear as mature sexual beings and adult women are infantilized. It is tragic but not surprising that these factors contribute to the sexual victimization of children. In addition, the intracontinuum effect relates to how, via these gender constructs, girls and women are reduced to sex objects. As objects, individuals are fragmented into sexual parts and humanity is stripped away. This process of dehumanization is a major force that allows perpetrators to rationalize sexual violence against women and girls.

Sexual abuse and violence are a particularly damaging consequence of sexualization, and the trauma that results from enduring this type of victimization is significant. Among individual effects, victims can struggle with unproductive coping strategies and the derailing of healthy identity development and body boundaries throughout much of their lives. Though it has been suggested that victimization in childhood raises the likelihood of similar experiences in adulthood, I have problematized this cyclical violence argument. I suggest alternatively that risks for adulthood victimization may be amplified for girls who experience sexual abuse, particularly in childhood, for very specific reasons. Desperation leads child sexual abuse victims to try to escape home at an early age, which may place them in situations where they are on the streets and struggling to survive. Within a gendered context, some survival strategies—such as running away or turning to sex work—both expose girls and young women to more vulnerability and are criminalized. Not only do running away and prostitution heighten possibilities for exploitation and violence, but these are the only two categories in which girls are arrested more than boys. Compounding the injuries of victimization, when girls are arrested for these crimes, they begin what often ends up as a lifetime entanglement with the justice system but does little to heal their initial trauma.

Context

The first part of what has been a twofold agenda in this book was to show that the continuum of sexualization, without exception, is part of the lives of all girls and women. Put simply, it is a way of framing the current gender set-up, which is rooted in the preservation of the status quo of power relations in society. The second portion of my agenda was the concurrent argument that, although all women have experiences along the continuum of sexualization, not one of these experiences is exactly the same for any two individuals. The main reason for this is that even though the continuum manifests in personal experiences, it is deeply rooted in structural, overlapping contexts that include advantages and disadvantages related to race, class, and other social, cultural, political, and economic aspects, along with institutional conditions such as education, access to resources and services, and family. In order to provide an illustration of how the continuum of sexualization is contextually situated, in previous chapters I drew upon my in-depth interviews with women in two disenfranchised populations, those who worked as exotic dancers and those who had experienced homelessness. The matrix of marginalizations in the lives of women in both populations provided a textured discussion of context. Specifically, their marginalizations heightened the risks of the women to multiple and severe experiences along the continuum of sexualization. The sheer magnitude of disadvantages that coalesced in their lives made it a struggle for the women as children, teenagers, and then as young adults to avoid compounding effects of these vulnerabilities. Though I discussed both protective and risk factors that play a role in girls' resilience, it is much more difficult to mitigate the influence of risk factors for girls already mired deeply in disadvantage.

Perhaps there were times that the struggles of the most marginalized populations of girls I discussed seemed disconnected from the middle class or mainstream. How important could something like media influence really be, for instance, when we are talking about girls struggling for survival on the streets? Certainly, some aspects of media messages are disseminated through means that not everyone can afford, such as expensive, high-tech gadgets. But in no way do these limitations circumvent exposure to the messages of sexualization; it is difficult to elude this cultural imperative. Rather than being removed from certain influences because they are intent on navigating more vulnerable and high-risk circumstances, girls who are struggling on the margins may integrate these gendered constructions into their survival strategies. As I have addressed in the discussion of "sexual solutions to nonsexual problems," for girls with few material alternatives, sexualization is one of the only resources available. "Traumatized early in childhood, many adultified before their thirteenth birthdays, girls figured out that youth sexiness was a transferable commodity supported by a booming market" (Schaffner 2006, p. 103). As Schaffner adds about girls in detention:

> In this sense, the young women in corrections, who were growing up with few material alternatives, were sexualized from the outside, adopted sexualized images of themselves internally, and then defended these ideas as being simply their own youth culture. The result was a process in which young women facing non-sexual problems—such as trouble at school, trouble with peers, family trouble—devised sexual solutions to them. The combination of both influences, commodified externally and fetishized internally, resulted in some young women having distorted notions about the role of sex and gender in their adolescence. (p. 102)

So, there is a bit of a tightrope of understanding we must walk about the use of the continuum of sexualization tool to understand experiences of girls and women. Selected examples throughout this book neither represent nor negate the larger picture. Context creates a basis from which different experiences along the continuum emerge; yet the continuum of sexualization remains the common thread among these varied experiences. I cannot comprehensively speak of every category or demographic of girls and women in one book. Instead, I argue that my research and that of others I reference herein reaffirms the relevance of the continuum of sexualization. When the experiences of girls and women manifest again and again from within so many different contexts and situations and what surfaces are these basic connections of sexualization, the continuum is clearly a defining factor in shaping the lived experiences of all girls and women.

My findings about the lives of women who were homeless or who worked as exotic dancers have the capacity to be both inspirational and, conversely, demoralizing. At first it is inspiring, a testament to human will. Despite every obstacle, the women devoted their energy and drive to achieving their relationship and family goals. Rather than breaking their spirit and momentum, their typically traumatic childhood experiences only spurred on their dreams of a "normal" life. They acknowledged a desire to redirect destructive patterns they had observed in their families of origin, to prove they could live differently, or even "better." Yet it became clear fairly quickly that the reality would not mesh with the dream. Instead, the women became more and more mired in poverty and social exclusion, trapped with abusive men or engaged in survival strategies that maintained their vulnerable position. Their options were severely limited. And so a second reaction becomes that of demoralization. Despite nearly heroic efforts, these women could not succeed at achieving what, for many, is a fairly realistic goal. The direction of their lives as they left adolescence and entered adulthood did not provide them with stability or peace. Rather, it engendered desperate coping strategies, violence, and justice system involvement. Intimate relationships that the women were in perpetuated many of the same problems they had already experienced along the continuum of sexualization, such as sexual victimization and exploitation, economic instability, and drug and alcohol addictions. Within a structural context of marginalizations, the women's exclusion from social support and resources intensified along with emotional problems and physical danger. Generally, these lived experiences contributed to a downward spiral in which the women were unsuccessful at improving their life conditions. I have looked to Richie's (1996) "gender entrapment" theory as descriptive of the constraints in the lives of the women. The theory of gender entrapment links experiences along the continuum of sexualization, starting with gender socialization, or "culturally constructed gender-identity development" (Richie 1996, p. 4), violence in intimate relationships, and the dearth of beneficial livelihood options for marginalized women. Gender entrapment describes a set-up for failure, a recipe for an outcome that maintains disadvantaged populations of women in their current conditions.

Situating the continuum of sexualization within contexts of multiple marginalizations and considering gender entrapment foregrounds the cataclysmic failure to improve the lives of girls and women in society. The populations of girls and young women who are most immersed in these layers of disadvantage are the most obviously in need of attention. Again, they are an example of what happens when the outer, protective layers of privileged race, class, or social position are stripped away. These are the girls who are least likely, despite their desires and best efforts, to be protected from the worst life has to offer. However motivated they may be, initially, to overcome the odds against them, their resilience is chipped away by structural contexts and risk factors that overwhelm their personal dreams. They are most likely to be punished for status offenses such as running away or for prostitution or petty drug crimes, most likely to end up in the juvenile justice system, most likely to have their potential ripped out from under them. What is less obvious and more insidious are the ways we are failing all girls and the ways that within society all girls are at risk. There are many connections between all girls and the ways we fail to support them. By locating experiences along a continuum of sexualization, we can clearly conceptualize this stark reality.

This problem must be approached from many angles in order to change the direction in which current and future generations of girls are headed. I noted in Chapter 6 that the best case scenario in terms of a solution is a tandem top-down and bottom-up approach, in which social inequalities that put girls at risk along the continuum of sexualization are addressed along with programs that can foster individual and institutional change. Of course, for girls who ultimately end up in the juvenile justice system, many opportunities to prevent or intervene have already been missed. In a funded effort to examine female delinquency using focus groups with girls and young women involved in the juvenile justice system in ten California counties, researchers Bloom et al. (2003) found that

> the early sexualization of these young women was discussed in terms of molestation and sexual abuse histories, the lack of non-motherhood options, such as careers and education, and the need for young women to become sexual in order to obtain status. The comments from the girls and young women generally described their need for information about sexuality and family planning and their desire to talk about their emotional concerns about sexuality. (p. 133)

This finding reinforces the conclusion that delinquent girls have already experienced many of the points along the continuum of sexualization that I have identified throughout this book before they arrived in the juvenile justice system: early sexualization, sexual abuse, lack of sexual identity or information about their bodies, lack of resources or status. What more do we need to let us know where the gaps are in our attention to the development of healthy girls? How many research studies must we produce, and how many girls need to end up on the streets or in the juvenile justice system? As Chesney-Lind and Irwin (2008) state:

> Advocacy for more of this sort of programming is critical, since it is clear that the girls in the juvenile justice system cannot wait another generation for things to change. As their numbers increase daily in the detention centers and training schools . . . it is long past time to pay attention to girls. Imagine how different the juvenile justice system would look if we as a nation decided to take girls' sexual and physical victimization seriously and arrested the perpetrators rather than criminalizing girls' survival strategies and jailing them for daring to escape. (p. 182)

Prevention and intervention are vital to changing the lives of girls and women for the better, but these cannot occur without a seismic shift in societal ideology and attitudes—and addressing social inequalities is not as straightforward as pressing for or implementing programming. My outgoing appeal, then, is that how we let girls grow up is of social significance and relevance to everyone. This is not just a "girl problem." It affects and reflects every single one of us. It impacts families, education, children, the state of our nation, our political climate, our economic status, and our position in the global lens. Our indifference to girls in crisis is a barometer of our social and individual integrity. This is a social problem and a social (ir)responsibility, a degradation of humanity at a time in history when we have every resource and skill to advance our enlightenment. How will we choose to use our technology and knowledge as a nation? We face a fork in the road. Along one path, we can continue to reduce people to their lowest common denominator, their one-dimensional, superficial meanings, and reproduce these for our consumptive entertainment and enjoyment. This path will destroy us eventually, in the generations to come, as depth of spirit and soul are snuffed out when daily life becomes meaningless and without purpose. The other path is difficult; we have to challenge our belief systems, our positions of power, look inward while reaching out. But this results in gains that have longevity, as girls grow into identities rooted in strong character and fundamentally healthy growth, become productive members of society, and advance the world in beneficial ways.

I have argued that the continuum of sexualization concept is vitally important to a deeper understanding of women's gender identity development and sexual victimization along with adult experiences and choices, and it should be part of any discussion about the complexity of women's lived experiences. At the same time, I am invested in the hope that someday the continuum of sexualization will be unnecessary and obsolete. First, though, the experiences it encompasses must be alleviated. I argue that, despite our being so easily seduced by quick fixes and with our attention spans minimized as we engage with new technology and multitask, this is a time when we must stop and reassess. We must work hard to question dominant attitudes, cast our votes for policy change and programs for girls, refuse to support the obsession with girls and women's bodies or the products that exploit pornified images of these bodies, and prioritize the qualities of all humans that contribute to our enrichment rather than our degradation.

Appendix
Methods for Qualitative Interviews with Exotic Dancers and Homeless Women

Exotic Dancers

From March to November 2000, I conducted qualitative, in-depth interviews with twenty current and former exotic dancers in a southwestern metropolitan area. Initial contacts were made from a variety of sources, including my college students who knew club managers or worked as dancers. I then used snowball techniques to reach women by phone or in person at local exotic dance clubs to request, arrange, and conduct interviews. Once an initial contact was made, I requested an interview. Interviews took place at several different private and mutually convenient locations, including my university office, the home of the interviewee, or a local restaurant or bar. Lasting an average of two hours, interviews were tape-recorded, transcribed, and coded. I also followed up with phone calls, which helped me clarify my questions and provided the women with another opportunity to share information. Pseudonyms were used in all cases to protect the identities of the interviewees. Women self-identified their race/ethnicity as: one Hispanic/Hawaiian, one African American, one African American/Hispanic, two Puerto Ricans, one Mexican American, one Filipino/White, one native African, one Costa Rican/Sicilian, and eleven Caucasians. The ages of the women at the time of the interview ranged from 18 to 40, with an average age of 26 years. The ages when they had begun dancing ranged from 14 to 29, with an average age of 19.

Homeless Women

From September 2003 to January 2004, I conducted qualitative, in-depth interviews with twenty homeless women staying at one of two homeless centers in a southeastern metropolitan area. As part of a larger project funded by the NIJ (Project no. 2002WGBX0013) investigating violence and women's homelessness, interviews with this population were facilitated by community contacts. The two homeless centers utilized are affiliated, both falling under the umbrella of the provider of homeless services in this location. Case managers at the homeless centers were asked to identify women at the centers who had experienced some form of violence. The first twenty women who fit this criterion and agreed to be interviewed were the participants for this study. Such purposive sampling (Babbie 1995) was appropriate; in qualitative research, interviewees are often intentionally chosen for the specific perspectives and life experience they may have (Esterberg 2002). Interviews were arranged by the case managers, who set up mutually convenient meetings. Interviews took place in a private conference or sitting room on site at the homeless center. Each interviewee was paid ten dollars for her participation. Lasting an average of two hours, completed interviews were tape-recorded, transcribed, and coded. Pseudonyms also protected the identities of this group. The race/ethnicity of the interview participants included six African American, three Hispanic, one African American and American Indian, one Puerto Rican and African American, and nine Caucasian women. The ages of the interviewees at the time of the interview ranged from 19 to 62, with an average age of 40.

Analysis

For all the women, interviews were semistructured and based on a set of open-ended, guiding questions that corresponded to general topic areas. These topic areas included questions relating to background and childhood, family relationships both as a child and as an adult, intimate relationships, perceptions of gender identity and body, power and control, violence and abuse, and homelessness. It is important to note that semistructured, in-depth interviews are an effective way to study women and other marginalized groups

(DeVault 1999; Reinharz 1992), particularly because these types of interviews enable members of historically silenced populations of women to tell their stories (Esterberg 2002). Further, qualitative interviews are "particularly useful in gathering information about stigmatized, uncomfortable, or difficult areas in subjects' lives" (Richie 1996, p. 16). I remained open throughout the process to emerging patterns that might suggest additional questions to be incorporated that were not originally included.

A two-stage process of coding was utilized. First, open coding (Esterberg 2002) allowed me to identify the themes and patterns that emerged in the transcripts of the interviews. As themes became evident, I then focused on the organization of these themes. During this second phase, focused coding (Esterberg 2002), we revisited the transcripts line by line to solidify central categories as well as accompanying subthemes. Following Reinharz's (1992) suggestions for feminist research, my intention was to document the lives of the women I interviewed, explore the experiences of the women from their own point of view, and understand their choices and actions from within a larger social context.

Bibliography

ABA and NBA (American Bar Association and the National Bar Association). 2001. *Justice by gender: The lack of appropriate prevention, diversion and treatment alternatives for girls in the justice system.* Washington, DC.

Acker, Joan. 1990. "Hierarchies, jobs, bodies: A theory of gendered organizations." *Gender & Society* 4:139–158.

Alcoff, Linda Martin. 1996. "Feminist theory and social science: New knowledges, new epistemologies." Pp. 13–26 in *Bodyspace: Destabilizing geographies of gender and sexuality*, edited by Nancy Duncan. New York: Routledge.

APA (American Psychological Association Task Force). 2007. *Report of the APA Task Force on the Sexualization of Girls.* Washington, DC.

Arata, C. M. 1999. "Coping with rape: The roles of prior sexual abuse and attributions of blame." *Journal of Interpersonal Violence* 14:62–78.

Avni, N. 1991. "Battered wives: The home as a total institution." *Violence and Victims* 6:137–149.

Babbie, Earl. 1995. *The practice of social research.* Belmont, CA: Wadsworth.

Balsamo, A. 1997. *Technologies of the gendered body: Reading cyborg women.* Durham, NC: Duke University Press.

Bandura, Albert. 1973. *Aggression: A social learning analysis.* Englewood Cliffs, NJ: Prentice Hall.

———. 1977. *Social learning theory.* Englewood Cliffs, NJ: Prentice Hall.

———. 2002. "Selective moral disengagement in the exercise of moral agency." *Journal of Moral Education* 31:101–119.

Bandura, A., Underwood, B., and Fromson, M. E. 1975. "Disinhibition of aggression through diffusion of responsibility and dehumanization of victims." *Journal of Research in Personality* 9:253–269.

Barnett, Ola, Miller-Perrin, Cindy L., and Perrin, Robin D. 2005. *Family violence across the lifespan.* 2nd ed. Thousand Oaks, CA: Sage Publications.

Bartky, Sandra. 1990. *Femininity and domination*. New York: Routledge.
Bass, E., and Thornton, L. 1991. *I never told anyone: Writings by women survivors of childhood sexual abuse*. New York: HarperPerennial.
Becker, J. V. 1988. "The effects of child sexual abuse on adolescent sex offenders." Pp. 193–207 in *Lasting effects of child sexual abuse*, edited by G. E. Watt and G. J. Powell. Newbury Park, CA: Sage.
Belknap, Joanne. 2007. *The Invisible woman: Gender, crime and justice*. 3rd ed. Belmont, CA: Thompson Wadsworth.
Bloom, Barbara, and Covington, Stephanie. 2001. "Effective gender-responsive interventions in juvenile justice: Addressing the lives of delinquent girls." Paper presentation, Annual Meeting of the American Society of Criminology, Atlanta, GA.
Bloom, Barbara, Owen, Barbara, Rosenbaum, Jill, and Deschenes, Elizabeth Piper. 2003. "Focusing on girls and young women: A gendered perspective on female delinquency." *Women & Criminal Justice* 14:117–136.
Bonczar, Thomas P. 2003. *Prevalence of imprisonment in the U.S. population, 1974–2001*. Washington, DC: US Department of Justice, Bureau of Justice Statistics.
Bordo, Susan. 1993. *Unbearable weight*. Berkeley: University of California Press.
Briere, J. 2002. "Treating adult survivors of severe childhood abuse and neglect: Further development of an integrative model." Pp. 175–203 in *The APSAC handbook on child maltreatment*, 2nd ed., edited by J. E. B. Myers, L. Berliner, J. Briere, C. T. Hendrix, and T. A. Reid. Thousand Oaks, CA: Sage.
Brownmiller, Susan. 1975. *Against our will: Men, women, and rape*. New York: Ballantine Books.
Butler, Judith. 1990. *Gender trouble: Feminism and the subversion of identity*. New York: Routledge.
CASA (National Center on Addiction and Substance Abuse at Columbia University). 2003. *The formative years: Pathways to substance abuse among girls and young women ages 8–22*. New York.
CDC (Centers for Disease Control). 2009. "CDC report finds adolescent girls continue to bear a major burden of common sexually transmitted diseases." Press release. http://www.cdc.gov/.
———. 2010. "Youth risk behavior surveillance—United States, 2009." *Morbidity and Mortality Weekly Report* 59 (SS-5):1–142.
Chang, Iris. 1997. *The Rape of Nanking: The forgotten holocaust of World War II*. New York: Penguin Books.
Chapkis, Wendy. 1986. *Beauty secrets: Women and the politics of appearance*. Boston: South End Press.
Chen, X., Tyler, K., Whitbeck, L., and Hoyt, D. 2004. "Early sexual abuse, street adversity, and drug use among female homeless and runaway adolescents in the Midwest." *Journal of Drug Issues* 34:1–21.
Chesney-Lind, Meda. 1997. *The female offender: Girls, women and crime*. Thousand Oaks, CA: Sage Publications.
———. 2001. "What about the girls? Delinquency programming as if gender mattered." *Corrections Today* 63:38–45.

———. 2002. "Criminalizing victimization: The unintended consequences of pro-arrest policies for girls and women." *Criminology and Public Policy* 2:81–91.
Chesney-Lind, Meda, and Irwin, Katherine. 2008. *Beyond bad girls: Gender, violence and hype.* New York: Routledge.
Chesney-Lind, Meda, and Pasko, L. 2004. *The female offender: Girls, women and crime.* 2nd ed. Thousand Oaks, CA: Sage.
Chesney-Lind, M., and Rodriguez, N. 1983. "Women under lock and key." *The Prison Journal* 63, 47–65.
Cixous, H., and Clement, C. 1986. *The newly born woman.* Translated by B. Wing. Minneapolis: University of Minnesota Press.
Cole, C. 1993. "Resisting the canon: Feminist cultural studies, sport, and technologies of the body." *Journal of Sport & Social Issues* 17:77–97.
Connell, R. W. 1990. "The state, gender, and sexual politics." *Theory & Society* 19:507–544.
———. 1995. *Masculinities.* Oxford, UK: Policy Press.
Crowley, S. 2000. *The search for autonomous intimacy: Sexual abuse and young women's identity development.* New York: Peter Lang.
Daly, K. 1994. *Gender, crime and punishment.* New Haven, CT: Yale University Press.
Dasgupta, Shamita Das. February 2001. "Towards an understanding of women's use of non-lethal violence in intimate heterosexual relationships." VAWNet Applied Research Forum paper. www.vawnet.org.
Davis, N. J. 1999. *Youth crisis: Growing up in a high risk society.* Westport, CT: Praeger.
DeVault, Marjorie L. 1999. *Liberating method: Feminism and social research.* Philadelphia, PA: Temple University Press.
Diamond, I., and Quinby, L., eds. 1988. *Feminism & Foucault: Reflections on resistance.* Boston: Northeastern University Press.
Dietz, Tracy. 1998. "An examination of violence and gender role portrayal in video games: Implications for gender socialization and aggressive behavior." *Sex Roles* 38:425–442.
Dines, Gail. 2009. "Childified women: How the mainstream pornography industry sells child pornography to men." Pp. 121–142 in *The sexualization of childhood,* edited by Sharna Olfman. Westport, CT: Praeger Publishers.
———. 2010. *Pornland: How porn has hijacked our sexuality.* Boston: Beacon Press.
Dobash, Rebecca E., and Dobash, Russell P. 1998. *Rethinking violence against women.* Thousand Oaks, CA: Sage.
Driscoll, Catherine. 2002. *Girls: Feminine adolescence in popular culture and cultural theory.* New York: Columbia University Press.
Dull, D., and West, C. 1991. "Accounting for cosmetic surgery: The accomplishment of gender." *Social Problems* 1:54–69.
Eigenberg, Helen. 2001. *Woman battering in the United States: Till death do us part.* Prospect Heights, IL: Waveland Press, Inc.
Esterberg, Kristin G. 2002. *Qualitative methods in social research.* Boston, MA: McGraw Hill.

Ezzell, Matthew B. 2009. "Pornography, lad mags, video games and boys: Reviving the canary in the coal mine." Pp. 7–32 in *The sexualization of childhood,* edited by Sharna Olfman. Westport, CT: Praeger Publishers.

Fagan, Abigail. 2001. "The gender cycle of violence: Comparing the effects of child abuse and neglect on criminal offending for males and females." *Violence and Victims* 16:457–474.

Farley, Melissa. 2009. "Prostitution and the sexualization of children." Pp. 143–163 in *The sexualization of childhood,* edited by Sharna Olfman. Westport, CT: Praeger Publishers.

Ferraro, Kathleen. 2006. *Neither angels nor demons: Women, crime and victimization.* Boston: Northeastern University Press.

Filipas, Henrietta, and Ullman, Sarah. 2006. "Child sexual abuse, coping responses, self-blame, posttraumatic stress disorder, and adult sexual revictimization." *Journal of Interpersonal Violence* 21:652–672.

Fineran, Susan. 2002. "Adolescents at work: Gender issues and sexual harassment." *Violence Against Women* 8:953–967.

Finkelhor, D. 1994. "Current information about the scope and nature of child sexual abuse." *The Future of Children* 4:31–53.

Finkelhor, D., and Browne, A. 1985. "The traumatic impact of child sexual abuse: A conceptualization." *American Journal of Orthopsychiatry* 55:530–541.

Fisher, S. 1973. *Body consciousness: You are what you feel.* Upper Saddle River, NJ: Prentice Hall.

Foubert, J. D., and McEwen, M. K. 1998. "An all-male rape prevention peer education program: Decreasing fraternity men's behavioral intention to rape." *Journal of College Student Development* 39:548–556.

Foucault, Michel. 1985. *The history of sexuality, volume two: The use of pleasure.* New York: Pantheon.

———. 1988a. *Madness and civilization.* 2nd ed. New York: Vintage Books.

———. 1988b. "Technologies of the self." Pp. 16–49 in *Technologies of the self: A seminar with Michel Foucault,* edited by L. H. Martin, H. Gutman, and P. H. Hutton. Amherst: University of Massachusetts Press.

———. 1990. *The history of sexuality: Volume 1: An introduction.* 2nd ed. New York: Vintage Books.

———. 1995. *Discipline and punish.* 2nd ed. New York: Vintage Books.

Gaarder, Emily, and Belknap, Joanne. 2002. "Tenuous borders: Girls transferred to adult court." *Criminology* 40:481–517.

Gilfus, M. E. 1992. "From victims to survivors to offenders: Women's routes of entry and immersion into street crime." *Women and Criminal Justice* 4:63–90.

———. 2006. "From victims to survivors to offenders: Women's routes of entry and immersion into street crime." Pp. 5–14 in *In her own words: Women offenders' views on crime and incarceration,* edited by Leanne F. Alarid and Paul Cromwell. Los Angeles: Roxbury.

Gilligan, James. 2007. *Violence.* New York: Vintage Books.

Girls' Justice Initiative. 2003. *Girls in the juvenile justice system:*

Perspectives on services and conditions of confinement. www.girls justiceinitative.org.

Giroux, Henry A. 1996. *Fugitive cultures: Race, violence, and youth.* New York: Routledge.

Gordon, Avery. 1997. *Ghostly matters: Haunting and the sociological imagination.* Minneapolis: University of Minnesota Press.

Griffin, Susan. 1981. *Pornography and silence.* New York: Harper & Row Publishers.

Hardesty, Jennifer L. 2002. "Separation assault in the context of postdivorce parenting: An integrative review of the literature." *Violence Against Women* 8:597–621.

Harlow, C. W. 1999. *Prior abuse reported by inmates and probationers.* Washington, DC: US Department of Justice, Office of Justice Programs.

Harvey, D. 1989. *The condition of postmodernity.* Oxford, UK: Blackwell.

Heger, Astrid, Ticson, Lynne, Velasquez, Oralia, and Bernier, Rapale. 2002. "Children referred for possible sexual abuse." *Child Abuse and Neglect* 26:645–659.

Heise, Lori L. 1998. "Violence against women: An integrated ecological framework." *Violence Against Women* 4:262–290.

Herman, J. 1997. *Trauma and recovery: The aftermath of violence—From domestic abuse to political terror.* New York: Basic Books.

Heywood, L. 1997. "Masculinity vanishing: Bodybuilding and contemporary culture." Pp. 165–183 in *Building bodies*, edited by P. Moore. New Brunswick, NJ: Rutgers University Press.

HGHW (Collaborative Fund for Healthy Girls/Healthy Women). 2001. *The new girls' movement: Implications for youth programs.* New York: Ms. Foundation for Women.

Hill-Collins, Patricia. 2008. *Black feminist thought.* New York: Routledge.

Hinshaw, Stephen. 2009. *The triple bind: Saving our teenage girls from today's pressures.* New York: Ballatine Books.

Hollander, Jocelyn A. 2001. "Vulnerability and dangerousness: The construction of gender through conversations about violence." *Gender & Society* 15:83–109.

Holmlund, C. 1997. "Visible difference and flex appeal: The body, sex, sexuality and race in the *Pumping Iron* films." Pp. 87–102 in *Building bodies*, edited by P. Moore. New Brunswick, NJ: Rutgers University Press.

hooks, bell. 1997. "Selling hot pussy: Presentations of black female sexuality in the cultural marketplace." Pp. 113–128 in *Writing on the body*, edited by K. Conboy, N. Medina, and S. Stanbury. New York: Columbia University Press.

———. 1999. *Black looks: Race and representation.* Boston: South End Press.

Impett, E. A., Schooler, D., and Tolman, D. L. 2006. "To be seen and not heard: Femininity ideology and adolescent girls' sexual health." *Archives of Sexual Behavior* 21:628–646.

Irigaray, Luce. 1985a. *This sex which is not one.* Translated by C. Porter. Ithaca, NY: Cornell University Press.

———. 1985b. *Speculum of the other woman.* Translated by G. Gill. Ithaca, NY: Cornell University Press.
Janus, Mark, McCormack, Arlene, Burgess, Ann W., and Hartman, Carol. 1987. *Adolescent runaways: Causes and consequences.* Lexington, MA: Lexington Books.
Jasinski, Jana L., Wesely, Jennifer K., Wright, James D., and Mustaine, Elizabeth E. 2010. *Hard lives, mean streets: Violence in the lives of homeless women.* Boston: Northeastern University Press.
Johnson, Michael P. 2000. "Conflict and control: Images of symmetry and asymmetry in domestic violence." In *Couples in conflict,* edited by A. Booth, A. C. Crouter, and M. Clements. Hillsdale, NJ: Erlbaum.
Josselson, R. 1987. *Finding herself: Pathways to identity development in women.* San Francisco: Jossey-Bass.
———. 1996. *Revising herself: The story of women's identity from college to midlife.* New York: Oxford University Press.
Kaw, E. 1998. "Medicalization of racial features: Asian-American women and cosmetic surgery." Pp. 166–183 in *The politics of women's bodies: Sexuality, appearance and behavior,* edited by Rose Weitz. New York: Oxford University Press.
Kilbourne, Jean. 1987. *Still killing us softly.* Cambridge, MA: Cambridge Documentary Films. Film.
———. 2000. *Killing us softly 3.* Northampton, MA: Media Education Foundation. Film.
———. 2010. *Killing us softly 4.* Northampton, MA: Media Education Foundation. Film.
Kimmel, Michael S., and Messner, Michael A. 2009. *Men's lives.* 8th ed. Boston: Allyn & Bacon.
LaFont, Suzanne. 2003. *Constructing sexualities: Readings in sexuality, gender and culture.* Upper Saddle River, NJ: Prentice Hall.
Lareau, Annette. 2003. *Unequal childhoods: Class, race and family life.* Berkeley: University of California Press.
Leban, Lexi, and Szajko, Lidia. 2004. *Girl trouble.* San Francisco: Critical Images. Film.
Lee, J. 1998. "Menarche and the (hetero)sexualization of the female body." Pp. 82–99 in *The politics of women's bodies,* edited by Rose Weitz. New York: Oxford University Press.
Levin, Diane. 2009. "So sexy, so soon: The sexualization of childhood." Pp. 75–88 in *The sexualization of childhood,* edited by Sharna Olfman. Westport, CT: Praeger Publishers.
Levy, Ariel. 2005. *Female chauvinist pigs: Women and the rise of raunch culture.* New York: Free Press.
Linn, Susan. 2009. "A royal juggernaut: The Disney princesses and other commercialized threats to creative play and the path to self-realization for young girls." Pp. 33–50 in *The sexualization of childhood,* edited by Sharna Olfman. Westport, CT: Praeger Publishers.
Lipsey, M. 1990. *Juvenile delinquency treatment: A meta-analytic inquiry into the variability of effects.* New York: Russell Sage Foundation.

Lorber, Judith. 1997. *Gender and the social construction of illness.* Thousand Oaks, CA: Sage Publications.

———. 1998. *Gender inequality: Feminist theories and politics.* Los Angeles: Roxbury.

Lydon, M. 1988. "Foucault and feminism: A romance of many dimensions." Pp. 139–150 in *Feminism & Foucault: Reflections on resistance,* edited by I. Diamond and L. Quinby. Boston: Northeastern University Press.

Madriz, Esther. 1997. *Nothing bad happens to good girls.* Berkeley: University of California Press.

Maine, Margo. 2009. "Something's happening here: Sexual objectification, body image distress, and eating disorders." Pp. 63–74 in *The sexualization of childhood,* edited by Sharna Olfman. Westport, CT: Praeger Publishers.

Marable, Manning. 2004. "Racism and sexism." Pp. 160–165 in *Race, class and gender in the United States,* 6th ed., edited by Paula S. Rothenberg. New York: Worth Publishers.

Martin, Emily. 1992. *The woman in the body.* Boston: Beacon Press.

McCormack, Arlene, Janus, Mark-David, and Burgess, Ann. 1986. "Runaway youths and sexual victimization: Gender differences in an adolescent runaway population." *Child Abuse & Neglect* 10:387–395.

McLorg, P., and Taub, D. 1987. "Anorexia nervosa and bulimia: The development of deviant identities." *Deviant Behavior* 8:177–189.

Messerschmidt, James. 1993. *Masculinities and crime: Critique and reconceptualization of theory.* Lanham, MD: Rowman & Littlefield Publishers.

Messman-Moore, T. L., Long, P. J., and Siegfried, N. J. 2000. "The revictimization of child sexual abuse survivors: An examination of the adjustment of college women with child sexual abuse, adult sexual assault, and adult physical abuse." *Child Maltreatment* 5:18–27.

Messner, Michael. 2002. *Taking the field: Women, men & sports.* Minneapolis: University of Minnesota Press.

Messner, Michael, and Sabo, Donald. 1994. *Sex, violence and power in sports: Rethinking masculinity.* Freedom, CA: Crossing Press.

Miller, Jody. 1998. "Up it up: Gender and the accomplishment of street robbery." *Criminology* 36:37–66.

———. 2008. *Getting played: African American girls, urban inequality and gendered violence.* New York: New York University Press.

Miller, Jody, and Brunson, R. K. 2000. "Gender dynamics in youth gangs: A comparison of male and female accounts." *Justice Quarterly* 17:801–830.

Miller, Jody, and Decker, S. H. 2001. "Young women and gang violence: An examination of gender, street offending and violent victimization in gangs." *Justice Quarterly* 18:115–140.

Miller, Jody, and White, Norman A. 2004. "Situational effects of gender inequality on girls' participation in violence." Pp. 167–190 in *Girls' violence: Myths and realities,* edited by C. Alder and A. Worrall. Albany: State University of New York Press.

Monto, M., and Hotaling, N. 2001. "Predictors of rape myth acceptance among male clients of female street prostitutes." *Violence Against Women* 7:275–293.

Morgan, K. P. 1998. "Women and the knife: Cosmetic surgery and the colonization of women's bodies." Pp. 147–166 in *The politics of women's bodies: Sexuality, appearance and behavior*, edited by Rose Weitz. New York: Oxford University Press.

Morris, Edward W. 2007. "Researching race: Identifying a social construction through qualitative methods and an interactionist perspective." *Symbolic Interaction* 30:409–425.

Murdoch, J. B. 2000. "Is imminence really necessity? Reconciling traditional self-defense doctrine with the Battered Women's Syndrome." *Northern Illinois University Law Review* 20:191–218.

Murthi, Meera, Servaty-Seib, Heather L., and Elliott, Ann N. 2006. "Childhood sexual abuse and multiple dimensions of self-concept." *Journal of Interpersonal Violence* 21:982–999.

Nagle, Jill. 1997. *Whores and other feminists*. New York: Routledge.

National Child Traumatic Stress Network. 2004. *Trauma among girls in the juvenile justice system*. Washington, DC: Substance Abuse and Mental Health Service Administration and US Department of Health and Human Services.

Neumann, D. A., Houskamp, B. M., Pollock, V. E., and Briere, J. 1996. "The long-term sequelae of childhood sexual abuse in women: A meta-analytic review." *Child Maltreatment* 1:6–16.

Newman, David M. 2000. *Sociology: Exploring the architecture of everyday life*. 3rd ed. Thousand Oaks, CA: Pine Forge Press.

NIJ (National Institute of Justice). 2003. *Research on women and girls in the justice system*. Washington, DC: Office of Justice Programs.

Noll, Jennie G. 2005. "Does childhood sexual abuse set in motion a cycle of violence against women? What we know and what we need to learn." *Journal of Interpersonal Violence* 20:455–462.

OJJDP (Office of Juvenile Justice and Delinquency Prevention). 2004. *Detection and prevalence of substance use among juvenile detainees*. Washington, DC: Office of Justice Programs.

———. 2009. *Resilient girls—Factors that protect against delinquency*. Washington, DC: Office of Justice Programs.

Olfman, Sharna. 2009. "The sexualization of childhood: Growing older younger/growing younger older." Pp. 1–4 in *The sexualization of childhood*, edited by Sharna Olfman. Westport, CT: Praeger.

Olsen, Francis. 1996. "Do (only) women have bodies?" Pp. 209–226 in *Thinking through the body of the law*, edited by Pheng Cheah, David Fraser, and Judith Grbich. New York: New York University Press.

Opotow, Susan. 2001. "Reconciliation in times of impunity: Challenges for social justice." *Social Justice Research* 14:149–170.

Orenstein, Peggy. 1994. *Schoolgirls: Young women, self-esteem, and the confidence gap*. New York: Doubleday.

Owen, Barbara. 1998. *In the mix: Struggle and survival in a women's prison*. Albany: State University of New York Press.

Paolucci, Elizbeth Oddone, Genuis, Mark L., and Violato, Claudio. 2001. "A meta-analysis of the published research on the effects of child sexual abuse." *Journal of Psychology* 135:17–36.

Pettiway, Leon E. 1997. *Workin' it: Women living through drugs and crime.* Philadelphia: Temple University Press.

Phillips, Alex, and Daniluk, Judith C. 2004. "Beyond "survivor": How child sexual abuse informs the identity of adult women at the end of the therapeutic process." *Journal of Counseling & Development* 82:177–184.

Plumwood, V. 1993. *Feminism and the mastery of nature.* New York: Routledge.

Raphael, Jody. 2000. *Saving Bernice: Battered women, welfare and poverty.* Boston: Northeastern University Press.

———. 2004. *Listening to Olivia: Violence, poverty and prostitution.* Boston: Northeastern University Press.

———. 2007. *Freeing Tammy: Women, drugs and incarceration.* Boston: Northeastern University Press.

Raphael, Jody, and Shapiro, Deborah. 2001. *Sisters speak out: The lives and needs of prostituted women in Chicago: A research study.* Chicago: Center for Impact Research.

Reebye, P., Moretti, M., Wiebe, V., and Lessard, J. 2000. "Symptoms of posttraumatic stress disorder in adolescents with conduct disorder: Sex differences and onset patterns." *Canadian Journal of Psychiatry* 45:746–751.

Reid-Cunningham, Allison Ruby. 2008. "Rape as a weapon of genocide." *Genocide Studies and Prevention* 3:279–296.

Reinharz, Shulamit. 1992. *Feminist methods in social research.* New York: Oxford University Press.

Rennison, C. M., and Welchans, S. 2000. *Intimate partner violence.* NCJ Publication No. 178247. Washington, DC: US Department of Justice.

Rich, Adrienne. 1976. *Of woman born.* New York: W. W. Norton.

Richie, Beth E. 1996. *Compelled to crime: The gender entrapment of battered black women.* New York: Routledge.

———. 2000. "Exploring the links between violence against women and women's involvement in illegal activity." Pp. 1–13 in *Research on women and girls in the justice system.* NCJ Publication No. 180973. Washington, DC: US Department of Justice.

Ronai, Carol Rambo, and Ellis, Carolyn. 1989. "Turn-ons for money: Interactional strategies of the table dancer." *Journal of Contemporary Ethnography* 18:271–298.

Rothenberg, Paula S. 2007. *Race, class & gender in the United States.* 7th ed. New York: Worth Publishers.

Rubin, Lillian B. 1976. *Worlds of pain: Life in the working-class family.* New York: Basic Books.

———. 1994. *Families on the fault line.* New York: HarperCollins.

Rumgay, Judith. 1999. "Violent women: Building knowledge-based intervention strategies." Pp. 106–127 in *Good practice in working with violence,* edited by H. Kemshall and J. Pritchard. London: Jessica Kingsley Publishers.

Russell, D. 1995. "The making of a whore." *Violence Against Women* 1:77–99.

Schaffner, L. 2006. *Girls in trouble with the law.* New Brunswick, NJ: Rutgers University Press.

Schisgall, David, and Alvarez, Nina. 2007. *Very young girls.* Showtime. Film.

Silbert, M., and Pines, A. M. 1982. "Entrance into prostitution." *Youth and Society* 13:471–500.

Snyder, Howard N. 2000. *Sexual assault of young children as reported to law enforcement: Victim, incident and offender characteristics.* Washington, DC: US Department of Justice, Bureau of Justice Statistics.

Sommers, Evelyn K., and Check, James V. P. 1987. "An empirical investigation of the role of pornography in the verbal and physical abuse of women." *Violence and Victims* 2:189–209.

Steiner, H., Garcia, I. G., and Mathews, Z. 1997. "Posttraumatic stress disorder in incarcerated juvenile delinquents." *Journal of American Academy of Child and Adolescent Psychiatry* 59:1133–1143.

Sweet, Nova, and Tewksbury, Richard. 2000. "What's a nice girl like you doing in a place like this? Pathways to a career in stripping." *Sociological Spectrum* 20:325–343.

Tjaden, P., and Thoennes, N. 2000. *Full report of the prevalence, incidence, and consequences of violence against women: Findings from the National Violence Against Women Survey.* Washington, DC: National Institute of Justice and Centers for Disease Control and Prevention.

Tolman, Deborah L. 2002. *Dilemmas of desire: Teenage girls talk about sexuality.* Boston: Harvard University Press.

Tyler, Kimberly A., and Cauce, Ana M. 2002. "Perpetrators of early physical and sexual abuse among homeless and runaway adolescents." *Child Abuse and Neglect* 26:161–174.

Tyler, Kimberly A., Hoyt, Dan R., and Whitbeck, Les B. 2000. "The effects of early sexual abuse on later sexual victimization among female homeless and runaway adolescents." *Journal of Interpersonal Violence* 15:235–251.

Tyler, Kimberly A., Whitbeck, Les B., Hoyt, Dan R., and Cauce, Ana Maria. 2004. "Risk factors for sexual victimization among male and female homeless runaway youth." *Journal of Interpersonal Violence* 19:503–520.

United Way of the Bay Area and the San Francisco Juvenile Probation Department. 2003. *Girls on the edge: A report on girls in the juvenile justice system.* San Francisco.

US Department of Justice. 2003. *Research, practice and guiding principles for women offenders: Gender-responsive strategies.* Washington, DC: National Institute of Corrections.

———. 2005. *Crime in the United States 2004.* Uniform Crime Reports. Federal Bureau of Investigation. Washington, DC: US Government Printing Office.

Weitz, Rose. 1998. "A history of women's bodies." Pp. 3–11 in *The politics of women's bodies,* edited by Rose Weitz. New York: Oxford University Press.

Wesely, Jennifer K. 2001. "Negotiating gender: Bodybuilding and the natural/unnatural continuum." *Sociology of Sport Journal* 18:162–180.

———. 2002. "Growing up sexualized: Issues of power and violence in the lives of female exotic dancers." *Violence Against Women* 8:1182–1207.

———. 2003. "Exotic dancing and the negotiation of identity: The multiple uses of body technologies." *Journal of Contemporary Ethnography* 32:643–669.

———. 2006. "Considering the context of women's violence: Gender, lived experiences and cumulative victimization." *Feminist Criminology* 1:303–328.

———. 2009. "'Mom said we had a money maker': Sexualization and survival contexts among homeless women." *Symbolic Interaction* 32:91–105.

Wesely, Jennifer K., and Gaarder, Emily. 2004. "The gendered 'nature' of the urban outdoors: Women negotiating fear of violence." *Gender & Society* 18:645–663.

Wesely, Jennifer K., and Wright, James D. 2009. "From the inside out: Efforts by homeless women to disrupt cycles of crime and violence. *Women & Criminal Justice* 19:217–234.

West, Candace, and Zimmerman, D. 1987. "Doing gender." *Gender & Society* 1:125–151.

West, Carolyn. 2009. "Still on the auction block: The (s)exploitation of black adolescent girls in rap(e) music and hip-hop culture." Pp. 89–102 in *The sexualization of childhood,* edited by Sharna Olfman. Westport, CT: Praeger Publishers.

West, Traci. 1999. *Wounds of the spirit: Black women, violence and resistance ethics.* New York: New York University Press.

Whitbeck, Les B., and Hoyt, Dan R. 1999. *Nowhere to grow: Homeless and runaway adolescents and their families.* New York: Aldine de Gruyter.

———. 2002. "Midwest Longitudinal Study of Homeless Adolescents: Baseline Summary Report for all Participating Agencies." Department of Sociology, University of Nebraska–Lincoln.

Whitbeck, Les B., Hoyt, Dan R., Yoder, Kevin A., Cauce, Ana Mari, and Paradise, Matt. 2001. "Deviant behavior and victimization among homeless and runaway adolescents." *Journal of Interpersonal Violence* 16:1175–1204.

Whitbeck, Les B., and Simons, Ronald L. 1990. "Life on the streets: The victimization of runaway and homeless adolescents." *Youth and Society* 22:108–125.

Widom, Cathy S. 1989a. "The cycle of violence." *Science* 244:160–166.

———. 1989b. "Child abuse, neglect and adult behavior: Research design and findings on criminality, violence and child abuse." *American Journal of Orthopsychiatry* 59:355–367.

———. 1989c. "Does violence beget violence? A critical examination of the literature." *Psychological Bulletin* 106:3–28.

———. 1992. "The cycle of violence. Research in brief." Washington, DC: National Institute of Justice, US Department of Justice.
Williams, L. 1997. "A provoking agent: The pornography and performance art of Annie Sprinkle." Pp. 360–379 in *Writing on the body,* edited by K. Conboy, N. Median, and S. Stanbury. New York: Columbia Unversity Press.
Wyatt, Gail E., Newcomb, Michael D., and Riederle, Monika H. 1993. *Sexual abuse and consensual sex.* Newbury Park, CA: Sage.
Yoder, Janice D. 2006. *Women and gender: Making a difference.* 3rd edition. Upper Saddle River, NJ: Prentice Hall.
Young, Iris. 1980. "Throwing like a girl: A phenomenology of feminine body comportment motility and spatiality." *Human Studies* 3:137–168.

Index

Abuse. *See* Childhood sexual abuse; Sexual abuse; Substance abuse; Victimization
Addiction, 15, 88, 143. *See also* Substance abuse
Adultification. *See* Age compression
Adverse effects: on healthy gender development, 27
Advertising. *See* Media
African Americans, 38–40, 74, 86, 118, 147–148
Age compression, 24
American Psychological Association (APA) Task Force, 24, 56–57, 63, 112–113
Anorexia, 16. *See also* Eating disorders
APA Task Force. *See* American Psychological Association (APA) Task Force

Behavior dysfunctions, 70, 124
Body technologies, 22–23. *See also* Cosmetic surgery

Bulimia, 16. *See also* Eating disorders
Butler, Judith, 21. *See also* Gender, performance

CDC. *See* Centers for Disease Control
Centers for Disease Control (CDC), 61–62
Chesney-Lind, Meda, 36, 78, 107; with Irwin, 30, 118, 122–123, 130–131, 145. *See also* "Criminalized victimization"; Sexual capital
Childhood sexual abuse (CSA), 34–37, 65, 69–82; effects of, 69–71; SHARE, 50; treatment of, 124–133
Cixous, H., and C. Clement, 18. *See also* Phallocentric
Class inequalities, 46–47
Complex personhood, 32, 72. *See also* Gordon, Avery
"Confused bodies," 32, 60, 66,

163

139. *See also* Tolman, Deborah
Cosmetic surgery, 16, 18, 22. *See also* Body technologies
"Criminalized victimization," 78–79, 120, 129. *See also* Chesney-Lind, Meda
Criminal justice system, 51, 77, 81, 85, 95, 97–98, 120, 132–133. *See also* Law enforcement
CSA. *See* Childhood sexual abuse
Cumulative victimization, 80, 88, 99, 101, 105–106. *See also* Victimization; Wesely, Jennifer
"Cycle of violence" theory, 72–74, 118. *See also* Widom, Cathy

Darwin, Charles, 13. *See also* Theory of evolution
Dasgupta, Shamita, 80, 98. *See also* Ecologically nested framework
Dehumanization, 39, 67–68, 82, 140. *See also* Sexual objectification
Depression, 35, 57, 62, 70, 73, 77, 108, 120, 124–125
Development, stages of, 28–29, 113
Dines, Gail, 12, 14, 19–20, 24–27, 30, 62–63, 66, 68–69, 140. *See also* Pornland: How Porn Has Hijacked Our Sexuality
Disadvantage: communities with, 75; contexts of, 54, 84, 86, 88, 106; of exotic dancers, 41, 47–48, 91; females compared to males, 39; of girls, 38, 80, 118, 133, 141, 143; of homeless women, 49, 51, 94; relative to privilege, 5, 34; as a source of women's violence, 99–101
Disney, 27–28, 136. *See also* Giroux, Henry
"Doing gender," 21. *See also* West, Candace, and D. Zimmerman
Domestic violence, 72, 76, 80, 102, 106. *See also* Victimization; Intimate partner violence
Dualism, 11

Early independence, 36–37, 47, 51–53, 75, 84
Eating disorders, 16, 57, 62, 70, 124; anorexia, 16; bulimia, 16
Ecologically nested framework, 98. *See also* Dasgupta, Shamita
Education: as institution, 8, 26, 141; jobs and budgeting skills, 118; lack of, 42, 47–48, 80, 133, 138, 144–145; of media literacy, 113. *See also* Girls Education and Mentoring Services (GEMS) program; Sexual education
Embodiment, 4, 8, 11–14; female 12, 20, 33, 72; performance of sexualized, 14–17, 136
Empty families. *See* Schaffner, Laurie
Essentialism, 8, 13

Exotic dancers: case study of, 41–48, 53–54
Exploitation, 24, 36, 54, 75, 81, 100–101. *See also* Victimization

Family dysfunction, 80
Fear: from abuse, 97; for life, 105; about safety, 119; of sexual victimization, 92; of violence, 87
Feminism, 10, 21
Ferraro, Kathleen, 74, 82, 84, 86–87, 107
Foster care, 13, 48
Foucault, Michel, 13, 19–22, 56; feminist criticism of, 19–20
Fractured identities, 21

GEMS. *See* Girls Education and Mentoring Services (GEMS) program
Gender: constructs, 11, 13, 21, 112, 121, 140; development, 27, 32, 107; expectations, 8–9, 19, 23, 27, 32, 137; identity, 3–5, 7, 9–14, 21, 29, 71, 107, 111–112, 126, 143, 148; inequality, 6, 11, 20, 38, 48, 76, 79, 95, 110; norms, 8–9, 22, 112; performance, 8–9, 15, 17–18, 21, 32, 58, 63–64; roles, 27–28, 80, 98; socialization, 3–5, 7–15, 18–19, 63, 79, 107, 110, 135–136
Gendered power imbalances, 79
Gendered violence, 27, 38
Gender entrapment, 106–107, 118, 120, 129, 143. *See also* Richie, Beth

Getting Played: African American Girls, Urban Inequality and Gendered Violence, 38. *See also* Miller, Jody
Girls Education and Mentoring Services (GEMS) program, 127
Girl Trouble film, 77–78, 117, 121
Giroux, Henry, 27–28. *See also* Disney
Gordon, Avery, 32, 72. *See also* Complex personhood

Hard Lives, Mean Streets: Violence in the Lives of Homeless Women, 48, 52, 97, 107
Hierarchy: on the streets, 39
Hill-Collins, Patricia, 40
Hinshaw, Stephen, 3, 25, 57–58, 66. *See also* Prosti-tots
Homeless women: case study of, 48–54
hooks, bell, 40
Hypererotic, 39
Hypersexualized image, 19, 22, 27, 31, 137. *See also* Pornified sexualization

Identity. *See* Gender, identity; Self-concept
Incarceration, 81; of girls, 81–82; of women, 81–82, 107, 131. *See also* Programmatic needs
Institutions, related to organizational structure, 8. *See also* Education; Media
Intimate partner violence, 46,

105. *See also* Domestic violence
"Intracontinuum effect," 62–63, 140
Irigaray, Luce, 18. *See also* Phallocentric

JJDPA. *See* Juvenile Justice and Delinquency Prevention Act
Juvenile detention. *See* Juvenile justice system
Juvenile Justice and Delinquency Prevention Act (JJDPA), 123
Juvenile justice system, 46, 77, 122, 126; detention in, 120, 126–132; girls in, 76, 79, 117, 128, 133, 145; problems with, 121, 122–124, 131, 144. *See also* Programmatic needs

Kilbourne, Jean, 24, 68. *See also Killing Us Softly* films
Killing Us Softly films, 68. *See also* Kilbourne, Jean

Lareau, Annette, 46
Law enforcement: experiences with, 91, 95–97, 101. *See also* Criminal justice system
Levy, Ariel, 3, 25, 32, 58, 64. *See also* "Raunch culture"
Lived experiences, 3–4, 21, 32, 37–40, 55, 60, 88–89, 135, 142–143, 146; case studies, 98, 103, 106; in childhood, 51, 84, 118; cumulative effects of, 107; exotic dancers, 41, 48, 91; homeless women, 48–50

Marginalization, 75, 81, 99, 106, 115, 119, 133, 141; class, 47, 49, 53; gender, 75, 106, 115, 119, 133, 141; intersections of, 34, 40, 87, 112, 115; structural, 38, 89, 143
Media, 8–9, 23–32, 39, 65, 112, 137–139, 141; literacy, 112–113; sexist, 27
Mental health: needs, 124; problems, 57, 124; treatment, 118
Midwest Longitudinal Study of Homeless Adolescents (MJSHA), 50
Miller, Jody, 38–39, 74–75, 117. *See also Getting Played: African American Girls, Urban Inequality and Gendered Violence*
Misogyny, 13, 39
MJSHA. *See* Midwest Longitudinal Study of Homeless Adolescents
Molestation, 35, 44–45, 63, 144. *See also* Victimization
"Moral exclusion," 67. *See also* Opotow, Susan
Ms. Foundation for Women's Collaborative Fund for Healthy Girls/Healthy Women, 111

National Institute of Justice (NIJ), 48, 148
National Violence Against Women Survey, 35
The New Girls' Movement, 110–111
NIJ. *See* National Institute of Justice

Opotow, Susan, 67–68. *See also* "Moral exclusion"
Oppression, 10–13, 21, 38–39, 59, 79, 114
Orenstein, Peggy, 57, 60, 139. *See also* "Sexual entitlement"

Panhandling, 37
Panopticon, 19; panoptical surveillance, 20
Parentified child. *See* Schaffner, Laurie
Pathways approach, 5, 120
Patriarchy, 10–11, 18, 79–80, 98
Perpetration, 5, 66, 73–74, 98–99, 106; of all crime, 79; of violence, 79, 80, 102
Pettiway, Leon, 53. *See also* "Structured choices"
Phallocentric, 18. *See also* Irigaray, Luce; Cixous, H., and C. Clement
Pornified sexualization, 4, 23, 29, 31, 33, 36, 41, 55–59, 62–66, 69, 79, 82, 110, 112, 115, 137–139. *See also* Hypersexualized image
Pornland: How Porn Has Hijacked Our Sexuality, 25. *See also* Dines, Gail
Pornography: porn culture, 19; pornified sexual image, 26, 40; pornographic media, 25; pornographic objects, African American women as, 40
Postmodernism, 21; postmodern feminists, 22, 32
Post-traumatic stress disorder (PTSD), 70, 73, 82, 124, 130

Privilege, 5, 11–12, 33–34, 54, 111–112, 114. *See also* Privileged lifestyles
Privileged lifestyles, 54, 143
Programmatic needs, 120, 126–127, 129–130, 133; for delinquent girls in juvenile justice system, 126–131
Prosti-tots, 25, 57. *See also* Hinshaw, Stephen
Prostitution, 25, 36–37, 39, 52, 76, 78, 118, 126–127, 140, 144
Pseudonyms, use of, 147–148
Psychosocial framing of adolescence, 80
PTSD. *See* Post-traumatic stress disorder
Purposive sampling, 148

Qualitative interviews, 40; with exotic dancers, 41; with female incarcerated offenders, 82, 86; with female prostitutes, 76, 127; with homeless women, 48, 74

Race: racial inequality, 38–39; racism, 28, 38–40, 77
Rape, 40, 44, 63, 69, 89–90. *See also* Victimization
Raphael, Jody, 37–39, 79, 81, 87, 108
"Raunch culture," 25. *See also* Levy, Ariel
Richie, Beth, 78, 86, 97, 106–107, 118, 143, 149. *See also* Gender entrapment
"Risk amplification," 36, 75
Rubin, Lillian, 46

Schaffner, Laurie, 12–13, 38, 73, 77, 99, 117, 126; empty families, 46, 85–86; parentified child, 85; sexual solutions to nonsexual problems, 36, 52, 94, 142
Seattle Homeless Adolescent Research and Education Project (SHARE), 50. *See also* Childhood sexual abuse
Self-concept, 4, 72, 79. *See also* Gender identity
Self-esteem, 57–58, 62, 110
Self-sexualization, 56
Sexist media, 27
Sexual abuse, 3, 5, 34; effects of, 69–71; treatment of, 124–133; and violence, 34–37. *See also* Victimization
Sexual addiction, 42
Sexual capital, 37. *See also* Chesney-Lind, Meda
Sexual degradation, 48–49, 77
Sexual desire, 31, 57–60, 66–67, 137–138
Sexual education, 30–31, 59–60, 113–114, 128, 137; abstinence, 30, 114; comprehensive, 114, 137
"Sexual entitlement," 57. *See also* Orenstein, Peggy
Sexual harassment, 69, 75, 80. *See also* Victimization
Sexualized appearance, 4, 15, 19, 41, 64, 140
Sexualized behavior, 2, 4, 31, 70
Sexualized performance, 2, 24, 57–58, 64–65
Sexual objectification, 14–29, 41–54, 66–67; of exotic dancers, 41–48, 53–54; of homeless women, 48–54. *See also* Dehumanization
Sexual solutions to nonsexual problems. *See* Schaffner, Laurie
Sexual violence. *See* Victimization
SHARE. *See* Seattle Homeless Adolescent Research and Education Project
"Silent bodies," 60. *See also* Tolman, Deborah
Social constructions, 10, 60, 79, 114
Social control, 9–10, 63, 88, 121–122
Social exclusion, 34, 40, 49, 51–53, 74, 80–85, 103, 115–117, 131, 143
Spears, Britney, 24–25
Sprinkle, Annie, 22
Stage performance, 1, 4, 13, 31
Stereotypes, 79; of gender, 9; of sexual availability, 79; of weakness, 79
Structural inequalities, 21, 38
"Structured choices," 53. *See also* Pettiway, Leon
Substance abuse, 15, 36, 70, 72, 132; as coping strategy, 128; treatment of, 118, 129, 132; as weight control, 15
Suicide, 70, 73, 80, 90, 124, 130
Survival sex, 36, 78, 93, 118, 131
Survival strategies, 37, 52, 77, 79, 98, 120, 140, 142–143, 145. *See also* Survival sex

Technologies of the self, 21. *See also* Foucault, Michel

Television, 25–27. *See also* Media
Theory of evolution, 13. *See also* Darwin, Charles
Tolman, Deborah, 3, 32, 58–60, 66–67, 114, 139. *See also* "Confused bodies"; "Silent bodies"
Trauma, 120; childhood, 13, 129; treatment, 125
Tweens, 28–29, 57, 137

Very Young Girls film, 126–127
Victimization, 5, 54, 75; domestic violence, 72, 76, 80, 102, 106; of exotic dancers, 89; of homeless women, 89; molestation, 35, 44–45, 51, 63, 144; rape, 35, 40, 44–50, 63–66, 69, 80, 85, 89–97, 101, 106, 138; sexual abuse, 3, 5, 34–37, 44, 50–51, 54, 65, 69–82, 87, 93–94, 115–116, 124, 127, 130, 132, 140, 144; sexual assault, 34, 62, 71, 73; sexual harassment, 42, 69, 75, 80; sexual victimization, 35–36, 75, 88, 92, 94, 98, 107, 124, 128, 138–140, 143, 146. *See also* Cumulative victimization
Video games, 27, 136. *See also* Media
Violence. *See* Victimization
Violent resistance, 99–101
Vulnerability, 38, 54, 76, 100–101, 108, 140; to sexual victimization and exploitation, 67, 71–72, 92, 139

Welfare Reform Act, 132
Wesely, Jennifer, 19, 22, 74, 80, 118
West, Candace, and D. Zimmerman, 8, 21. *See also* Gender performance
Widom, Cathy, 73. *See also* "Cycle of violence" theory

Youthification. *See* Age compression

About the Book

It is often said that sex sells, but who pays the price? Jennifer Wesely probes the sources and consequences of sexualization in girls' and women's lives. Offering new insights into an enduring problem, she documents the increasingly pervasive and powerful nature of raunch culture and demonstrates how females are being sexualized in ways that are more extreme and damaging than ever before.

Jennifer K. Wesely is associate professor of criminology and criminal justice at the University of North Florida.

DATE DUE	RETURNED
APR 01 2013	MAR 26 2013
JAN 02 2014	JAN 06 2014
JAN 20 2014	FEB 07 2014
	MAR 19 2014
FEB 21 2014	MAR 11 2014
JUL 29 2014	JUL 22 2014
NOV 25 2015	DEC 09 2015
NOV 18 2016	NOV 17 2016